FileMaker 17 Manual for Novices

Richard Carlton & David Kachel

FileMaker 17 Manual for Novices

version 6.0x09 last updated 6-08-2018

© 2018 Richard Carlton

Published by Richard Carlton Consulting

Notice of Rights:

All rights reserved. No part of this book may be reproduced or transmitted in any form by any means, electronic, mechanical, photocopy, recording or other without the prior written permission of the publisher, except in the case of brief quotations embodied in critical reviews and certain other noncommercial uses permitted by copyright law. For permission requests, write to the publisher, LearningFileMaker.com / RCC, email: support@rcconsulting.com, 1805 N Carson St x-114, Carson City NV, 89701, USA.

Trademarked names, logos, and images may appear in this book. Rather than use a trademark symbol with every occurrence of a trademarked name, logo, or image we use the names, logos, and images only in an editorial fashion and to the benefit of the trademark owner, with no intention of infringement of the trademark. The use in this publication of trade names, trademarks, service marks, and similar terms, even if they are not identified as such, is not to be taken as an expression of opinion as to whether or not they are subject to proprietary rights.

FileMaker is a trademark of FileMaker, Inc., registered in the U.S. and other countries. FileMaker Pro, FileMaker Go, FileMaker Server, FileMaker WebDirect and the file folder logo are all trademarks of FileMaker, Inc. Richard Carlton Consulting - Nevada, LLC is an independent entity and this publication has not been approved by FileMaker, Inc.

Apple, the Apple logo, iPad, iPhone, iPod, iPod touch, iTunes, the iTunes logo, Mac, and QuickTime are trademarks of Apple Inc., registered in the U.S. and other countries. Multi-Touch is a trademark of Apple Inc. App Store is a service mark of Apple Inc. IOS is a trademark or registered trademark of Cisco in the U.S. and other countries and is used under license.

While the advice and information in this book are believed to be true and accurate at the date of publication, neither the authors nor the editors nor the publisher can accept any legal responsibility for any errors or omissions that may be made. The publisher makes no warranty, express or implied, with respect to the material contained herein.

ISBN-13: 978-1719179782 (Paperback)

Cover image designed by: Henry Mosiman

Interior Images by: Myles Debski

Lead Editor: Richard Carlton and Myles Debski

Assistant Editors: Rachel Young and Haylee Marie

Printed by CreateSpace an Amazon Company

Second printing edition

Richard Carlton Consulting Inc is a Nevada Corporation

1805 N Carson St x-114, Carson City NV, 89701, USA

Phone: 408-492-9701

E-mail: support@rcconsulting.com

Distributed to the book trade worldwide by LearningFileMaker.com

Contents

Preface	**X**
Video *Playlist*	**XI**
Author's *Note*	**XIII**
1 Fields and Variables	**1**
Global Fields	1
Private Global Fields	2
ID Fields	3
Primary Key Fields	4
Foreign Key Fields	5
Creation Date & Creation Time Fields	6
Repeating Fields	6
Unstored Calculation Fields	7
Lookup Fields	8
Field Validation	9
Hidden Utility Fields	10
Field Conventions	11
Field Name Pairs For Relationships	12
Naming Scripts	13
Cut & Paste Will Ruin Your Data	14
Where to Put Graphics Globals	14
Variables	15
Global Variables	15
Local Variables	16
Monitoring Variables	16

2 Layouts — 17

- Angry Fruit Salad 17
- Layout Size Consistency 18
- Object Jumping - "Pixel Shift" 19
- Fonts 19
- Field Label Colors 20
- Bold, Underline, Extend, Condensed, etc. 20
- Data Text vs Everything Else 20
- Visually Indicate Unuseable Items 20
- Field Elbow Room 21
- Grouping Like Data 21
- Familiar Object Locations 21
- Get Your Client's Logo Immediately 22
- Flashing 22
- Always Have an About Screen 23
- Startup Scripts 24
- Determine Window Size Before Creating Layouts 24
- Stay Off the Button and Graphic Bandwagon 26
- Finding Waldo (Overstuffing Layouts) 27
- Always Return Your User to Where He Left Off 28
- Drilling For Oil 28
- Don't Use FileMaker's Buttons as Tabs 29
- Be Sparing With Graphics 29
- Comments 30
- Apple's Human Interface Guidelines 30

3 Database Design — 32

- Don't Build a House Without a Blueprint 32
- An Object Lesson 35
- Reports — Build Them Last, Design Them First 40
- Lock Users Out of Everything 45
- Excessive Cleverness (everything on one layout) 47
- File Naming 48
- Don't Mix Techniques 49

Think Outside The Box 49

Programmer Control of Data Entry 51

Tab Based Layout Navigaton. 53

Data, Logic and Layout Design. 55

Remember That It's All About the Data 59

Custom Themes and Shared Styles 60

Leave a Trail of Bread Crumbs 61

Make Certain You Have at Least One Record 62

Test Your Solution Often 63

Watch for Gotchas 64

Table Occurrences 65

User Settings 66

Reports Tables 67

Random Number Generator 68

Closing Words on Database Design 72

4 Database Design Errors   73

Separate Printing Layouts. 73

Never Print a Portal. 73

Cute & Clever Tricks. 75

Chasing the Mouse 77

Don't Use Single-Step Buttons. 77

Orphans are Okay 78

Mile-Long Popups 81

Plugins 81

Window Confusion 83

Multiple Files and Data Separation. 85

Don't "Show Custom Dialog". 86

Title Case and Proper() are Improper 87

5 Scripts   89

Allow User Abort. 89

Don't Use Cut, Copy or Paste in Your Scripts 90

Don't Use AppleScript. 90

Error Trapping in Scripts. 91

Halt Script Steps 92

Prepare for Upgrades From Day One – Keeping your design structure Consistent . . . 93

Run Script With Full Access Privileges. 95

Startup & Shutdown Scripts 96

Startup Scripts are Required; Closing Scripts are Optional. 96

Robots 96

6   Dealing With Clients   101

Always Give Them More Than They Expect 101

Communicate With Your Client. .103

Don't Let the Client Design the Project 104

Feature Creep 105

Give Them What They Need, Not What They Want 107

Clients Should Never Look Over Your Shoulder. 109

The Client is Always Wrong 110

Think Like a Spy 112

Store Client Passwords in Three Places 113

Hacking the Password in FileMaker. 113

7   Don't Abuse FileMaker   115

Client File Integrity 115

Clients Will Not Perform Backups .117

Database Backup Strategy – FileMaker Cloud 118

Database Backup Strategy – FileMaker Server 119

Check Your Backups 120

Types of Corruption. 121

Detecting Corruption (Structural and Data) 122

Structural Corruption 122

Data Corruption 123

Final Notes about Corruption 124

8 *Tools* 126

    Bug & To-Do Tracking 126

    Building on a FileMaker server. 127

    Build a Tips & Techniques Database 128

    Create a Developer's Template 128

    Buy a Computer 129

9 *Techniques* 130

    The Correct Relational Graph 130

    Check Your Buttons. 131

    Technical Debt 132

    Impossible Data 132

    Alternate Methods of Dealing with Technical Debt. 138

10 *Gotchas* 140

    Mixing Versions of FileMaker 140

    Sending Email out of FileMaker 141

    Shared Hosting 141

    Runtimes 142

    Getting Old and Grumpy 143

    Web API Integration 143

11 *Miscellaneous* 146

    New Layouts. 146

    Wait, What Changed?. 146

    Another Case for Multiple Machines 147

    Limit the Time You Work on Your Solution. 147

    Building Commercial Software 148

    Notes from David (and endorsed by Richard) 149

    Building a Vertical Market Product .151

    FileMaker Certification 153

    API's Provided By FileMaker 154

12	**Critical Final Notes: Know Thyself & Know Thy Toolset**	**157**
	Reflect on the Reflection	.157
	Don't You Have Anything Positive to Say?	.157
	Pros/Cons of Working On a Live File	.159
	Pros/Cons of Working On an Offline File	.160
	All Is Not Lost	.160
	What Makes a Good FileMaker Developer?	.161
	The Social Side of the FileMaker Community	.161
	Final Note	.162

Other Resources — 164

About the Author — 165

Check Us Out — 166

Preface

FileMaker is an awesome tool!

As you read this manual, I highly recommend that you have access to my FileMaker 17 Video Course. This manual has been updated for the FileMaker 17 release, and having access to my 55 hours of video will GREATLY enhance your learning. If you do not have this video course, here is a 50% coupon. Go get it! This is not about me making money. It is about you learning.

If you have zero knowledge of FileMaker, then I am going to recommend a short list of videos that you should watch first. Once you have completed those, then you should start this manual. This list can be found on the next page. As an example, you should generally know what Fields are and conceptually know what Relationships and Variables are. In this book, we are going to tell you why you should use certain Fields or certain kinds of Variables under certain circumstances. We are not going to tell you what Fields and Variables are.

This book was written with the intent of keeping the novice out of trouble and from being forced to start a solution over from scratch. It is not to start a debate with every developer who believes he or she has a better or more sophisticated approach. For every problem to be solved in FileMaker, there are at least six solutions, all valid under the right circumstances.

This is not a front-to-back book. Entries are short bits of practical advice organized as best as possible in related groups.

I have worked hard to update this manual with the latest material. You are likely to find previous versions of this text as downloadable PDFs on the internet. However, much of the previous content is thoroughly out of date.

If you have questions or comments about the book, feel free to send them to support@rcconsulting.com.

All the best,

Richard Carlton

Video Playlist for brand new FileMaker Users, who want to get up to speed

Note: These videos are in our FileMaker 17 Platform Video Training Course

0105 - The FileMaker Platform - Summary

0110 - What kind of Solutions can be made with FMSP?

0107 - Product Positioning

0330 - Basics of Sharing a Database

0301 - Opening Files for New Users

0304 - What is a Database - Part 1

0305 - What is a Database - Part 2

0307 - Modes in FileMaker

0315 - What is a Relationship? (Very Basic Video)

0401 - Finding Records - Basics

0501 - Layouts - Available tools

0502 - Tour of the Inspector Pane

0503 - Tour of the Object Pane

0504 - Intro to Adding Fields to Database (Text & Number)

0901 - Scripting

0902 - Intro to Script Workspace

0909 - Variables vs. Globals

0801 - Calculation Engine & New Work Space

0802 - Calculation Engine & New Work Space Part 2

1101 - What is a Relationship?

1102 - Table Occurrence Basics

1201 - Security in FileMaker Overview

1501 - Deployment & Sharing Terminology

1502 - Deployment & Sharing Intro.

VIDEO TIP

Along the way, I will identify specific videos for you to watch to expound on the current topic. The easiest way to watch the video is to make a note of the video's four-digit number. Then watch that video to augment your learning in this book. Trust me! You are going to learn a lot!

Author's Notes

For the novice and intermediate developer, FileMaker 17 brings many great visual improvements. Specifically, the restructuring of layout mode with attached left and right panes is a welcome improvement. In previous versions of FileMaker, the inspector panel was always getting lost on my 27" monitor.

Additionally, FileMaker has opted to make sure that everyone who has FileMaker Pro actually has Pro Advanced! So now you (and everyone else) has access to Script Debugger, Data Viewer, and other important tools.

However, the long-term success of the FileMaker platform is tied to FMI's ability to modernize the platform while empowering the novice and intermediate developer to make great custom apps.

FileMaker has publicly discussed the direction it is taking towards modernizing and improving the process for updating, patching and migrating FileMaker solutions. Building a custom app is one skill set. Maintaining it, updating your users, and patching bugs are other equally important skills.

FileMaker is making good progress in this area. The FileMaker Data Migration Tool is an excellent example of FMI's investment toward improving the solution updating process. In fact, this new tool is the best and most important feature of the 17 release. That being said, this is a tool that new developers should probably ignore for now. Focus on learning the basics of building a good FileMaker solution. Just make a note in the back of your mind, that when you need to rapidly move data from an old FileMaker solution to an updated one, there is a new high-speed tool for this process. We discuss this more at the end of the book.

In terms of licensing for an office of FileMaker Users: FileMaker is moving to a model where they do not sell individual products. Gone are the days where you have to buy 4 copies of Pro, 2 copies of Pro Advanced and a copy of FileMaker Server with 10 connections. That was a complex process. When buying for a team of users, count the number of users and give that number to a FileMaker Sales Rep (or email my team). 8 People? No problem. You will receive a quote for 8 people to use FileMaker. Then, that group of 8 people will get access to ALL of FileMaker's products! Very Simple!

Of course, if you're a single user, you can still buy a single copy of FileMaker Pro Advanced for yourself.

FileMaker is on course to modernize the platform while simplifying licensing. Welcome improvements!

VIDEO TIP - 17 PLATFORM VIDEO COURSE

To learn more about panes, watch videos "0502 - Right Pane" and "0503 - Left Pane."

TERMINOLOGY

If you see the word "FileMaker", we are referring to the product or the platform.

If you see the word "FMI" we are referring to the hard-working company that makes the awesome product.

VIDEO TIP - 17 PLATFORM VIDEO COURSE

To learn more about "Data Migration" check out the 2400 section of videos in the FileMaker 17 Platform video course.

TERMINOLOGY

A file that you can access through the FileMaker App (on Mac or Windows) may be called a "Custom App," "Solution," "Database," or "Template." These terms mean the same thing in the FileMaker community. FileMaker Inc., periodically chooses to change the terminology to better address marketing and sales issues.

One last note about terminology. The official term when referencing this software, for all copies of FileMaker that now run on Mac and Windows is "Pro Advanced." There are only two problems with this. First off, writing out the full name burns and wastes a lot of text in this book. The second reason is that I have been calling this product "Pro" for 28 years. LOL.

So, for brevity, I will refer to "FileMaker Pro" or "FileMaker Pro Advanced" as "Pro."

This simplifies the writing, and the intent should be clear.

The FileMaker 17 Manual for Novices

1 Fields and Variables

Global Fields

Global fields are simple, and a great blessing. They were often used as variables in the distant FileMaker past, though there is little need for this particular application now that we have built-in variables (we cover variables in the next section). Still, globals are extremely beneficial, having many other uses and there are some vital things you need to know about them before you start coding.

Global fields are used when every record in a table requires access to exactly the same information. If the value of a field will always be the same for every record in a table and for every user, then a global field may be the ideal choice. It stores the information in one place only but treats it as though it were a field in every record. This eliminates unnecessary overhead and allows a more streamlined database.

Under some circumstances the data contained in globals can be lost, so beware. For example, when saving a clone of a file, the data in global fields is NOT saved with the clone. The global fields are saved empty, just like all the other fields, and if your database uses globals the way most do, your cloned database is useless until you import all that global field data back into the cloned database. This is a very good reason to make certain all global fields that fit this description are stored in the same table, so that only one import is needed and there is less likelihood of something getting left out by mistake.

A value in a global field will be accessible from any layout that belongs to that file, regardless of the table that you are viewing. I know that's a mouthful. The important thing to take away is that values in global fields are accessible within the current file and are not shared between FileMaker files. If you have a FileMaker solution that contains multiple files, then values in global fields will not be shared between files.

To learn more about Global Fields, watch video "0522 - Global Fields".

Private Global Fields

Global fields behave a bit differently when a database is set up to be accessed by multiple users, either through sharing or when accessed via server.

When a user logs into a database, all the globals on the server are effectively *copied* over so that each user gets a separate, private set of global field contents that are just for him and are no longer connected to the main database. These *copies* of the global fields vanish at logout and do not replace the original values on the server.

Many FMP newcomers are puzzled when they reach a point where they begin to try out their database(s) with multiple users. They discover that information contained in global fields is not correct when they sign in again after believing they had altered it before logging out. This is because there is one master set of globals contained in the actual file. The information contained in these fields is that which was placed there by the person who developed the database(s) or who last accessed it as a single user in order to change the global field content. When that file is shared so that other users can access it, whether by just turning on sharing in FMP, or by serving the files with FM Server (or FileMaker Cloud), each user gets a fresh set of private global fields that are loaded onto his machine at login with whatever information was originally contained in the master set before the file was shared. This means that any vital information that is different for each user cannot be stored in a global field because it would be lost at logout. The only way to change the information contained in the master set of globals is to open the database(s) as a single user (not by accessing through FM server). Only then can the information in global fields be changed for all users.

DO use global fields to store static information or graphic objects that will never change and will be the same for every record and user, such as a company logo that will appear on each layout.

DO use global fields as the primary key for a dynamic relationship such as a filtered portal (the user selects specific criteria which limit the records the portal can show).

DO NOT use global fields to store user settings. Each user will expect to find the same settings each time he logs in, but the data in his set of globals evaporates when he logs out. (User settings should be stored in a record created just for that user, in a table built specifically for this purpose. For example, in FM Starting Point, there is a Staff table where one user = one record. This is a great location to store user-specific settings. Each user gets a record of his own and all fields in these records are standard fields, not global.)

DO NOT store constants for calculations in globals if there is any possibility at all those constants might one day change and thereby alter

---

FYI

As an alternative, I frequently will use global fields and/or global variables to manage session settings for the user. A session setting is a setting that is specific to this user's interaction with the database, but is not something that would be saved with the staff record. I highly recommend that you use a startup script in your FileMaker solution that runs once each time a user opens the solution.

For more information on Startup Scripts, view Page 24 of this book.

archived records that are supposed to remain static. For example, you can store the value of pi in a global field. There is little chance that will change. But do not store constants such as a tax rate in a global field unless it will be *copied* into a separate non-global field before actual use. We all know what happens to tax rates!

ID Fields

You will see these referred to as primary key fields, ID fields, serial number fields, etc. They are unique identifiers for each record in a table. Every table needs them, no exceptions.

For every table you create, the first field in that table should always be a unique ID field. The best and only completely reliable way to do this is to create a text field that is auto-enter, serial number, increment by one, cannot override. This will be the single most reliable and predictable method to identify and relate your records.

The simplest way to name this field is by using the text "id_", and the name of the table, such as: id_contact, or id_invoice. Use exactly the same name for the matching foreign key in related tables.

No matter how certain you are that your primary key field(s) will be something else, always create an ID field of the type described above anyway. You will need it.

To better troubleshoot a database, I tend to put a three-digit Identifier ahead of the serial number. That way when your looking at primary keys, the first three or four digits of the serial number will tell you the table from where it originates. The serial number that is attached to the end of this identifier will ensure that this always remains unique.

Example: INV0005

On occasion, a client will demand a different type of identifying field. They may want their invoices to be identified by something like: 2017-INV-Smith. In these cases you can keep the client happy by creating a dummy ID field that contains what they want, and shows up where they want to see it, while doing the real work behind the scenes with your unique serial ID field. (Unjustified complexity always leads to disaster.)

One last thing. There is no reason for this field to appear on any layouts with user access, ever. You are never going to alter it, and it is just a record identifier.

VIDEO TIP - 17 PLATFORM VIDEO COURSE

To store constants for calculations or other Preference settings that are not specific to a user, use a Preferences or Settings table.

To learn more about a Preference Table, watch video "1141 - Preference Table in your Solution".

VIDEO TIP - 17 PLATFORM VIDEO COURSE

To understand the basics of ID fields and Relationships, watch video "0315 - What is a Relationship?".

Also found on YouTube:

https://youtu.be/WXJuSNyVcTs

TERMINOLOGY

Sometimes we say "Client." Sometimes we say "customer." To me, they mean the same thing. If you are a business major and grossly disagree with this, then please send a complaint email to the editor.

> **OPINION**
>
> Some developers prefer to actually display the unique ID fields on the layout. The essential element here is that the user can never edit or manually change that ID field. Feel free to go to the field Inspector and set the field to be non-enterable in Browse Mode, while being a field that may be entered in Find Mode. This allows you to actually display and find on the ID field without risk of your users changing the value.

In recent versions of FileMaker, there is a function to generate a UUID, which is a fancy way of saying a very random 32 digit number. I have never been super comfortable with this process because FileMaker is randomly generating a unique string and it is conceivable that FileMaker could generate the same string twice. That being said, FileMaker officially states that the chances of this happening are in the neighborhood of one in one billion.

Example: df114307-a600-456e-b7fc-3e8cfcbe7dec

As a more fundamental concept, if you use a serialized ID instead of a randomly generated UUID (like above), you will find triaging and troubleshooting relationship issues much simpler. Viewing a sequential group of records is self-evident if you use a unique serialized ID. For example:

INV0005
INV0006
INV0007

The same three records with a random UUID would probably look like this:

df114307-a600-456e-b7fc-3e8cfcbe7dec-6c2f4adc-ef0f-42ff-a68a-7d0179baf5bf-5b29dcb5-09b5-4baa-b0aa-9510025c033e

As you can see, there may be a benefit to seeing it one way over another.

TRAINING: For training purposes, I always prefer the serialized number. It is easier to understand. Updating a FileMaker solution where you have to import records, is dramatically easier if you are using auto-generated UUIDs.

Primary Key Fields

In a relational database, ID fields are frequently used as key fields. Key fields are the fields that drive a relationship.

There are lots of ways and reasons to create other kinds of key fields for your database, but many of them can lead to problems. You must be careful.

Concatenation fields in particular can be an enormous problem. These are calculation fields with a text result that displays one or more other fields. If you have first name and last name fields, you may try to create a unique identifier field that runs the two fields together, such as: JohnDoe. (Modern versions of FMP make this kind of relationship easier than it once was, but the basic problem is the same.)

It seems to make sense on the surface, until you realize that the minute you have two John Doe's in your database, your system is broken.

The first thought some people have is to add some other unique identifier to the concatenation. But then one discovers the problem becomes even more complex and uncertain.

Even FMP's timestamp can't be safely added to a key concatenation because two new records could conceivably be created at the same instant for persons with the same name. Alternatively, you might add the unique ID field described above, but this begs the question: "What's the point?" Why not just use that in the first place?

When creating key fields that use something other than a unique ID number, you must take pains to be certain there is no possibility of duplicate identifiers. This is far more difficult than it might seem.

As previously mentioned, some developers may try to use UUID, that will generate a random string.

In the long run, for intermediate and novice developers, it is much safer, smarter and more efficient to use the kind of field described above under ID Fields, unless you have a specific and compelling reason for using something else. Other types of key fields are best used for secondary functions such as filtering portals where they can't do any serious harm to your data if they fail.

> **OPINION**
>
> Absolutely! It is better to use unique ID fields, if there is any question. Keep in mind that one critical use of the UUID as a key field is when building a solution that requires offline synchronizatinon. If your sales team takes a local copy of the FileMaker solution offline onto their laptop, the regular unique ID field process won't work, because you will have two or three people all creating Invoice #100 and the invoices will be completely different. In an offline synchronization situation you will have to use UUID as a key field.

Foreign Key Fields

Foreign Key Fields are usually not an issue. It is probable that half or more of the relationships you are likely to create will automatically have a foreign key field populated by FileMaker, as it creates a related record. In a secondary situation where you're filtering a portal or creating a report (aka, the record pre-exists), then you may be auto-generating the foreign key field yourself. Keep in mind, in this situation, all the rules from the Primary Key Fields conversation are applicable here as well.

Make certain all of your foreign key fields are stored and fully indexed, otherwise your relationships will either not work, or will be very slow.

Creation Date & Creation Time Fields

Simple

Put one of each in every table, no exceptions. Sooner or later you will need them, most likely sooner. Name them *creationDate* and *creationTime* respectively. These are *auto-enter*, *non-modifiable*, date and time fields.

If you add them to your tables after the tables already contain records, the preexisting records will not contain creation date or time data and you will have to put it in manually. The first time you have to do this for a few hundred or a few thousand records will most assuredly cure you.

If you need modifiable, auto-enter date and time fields, *do not use these!* Make duplicates and use those. Then you have the best of both worlds.

Make certain your client knows his computers need to be connected to the internet and that all time and date preferences have to be set to retrieve those numbers from the internet. If a computer battery dies and this preference is turned off, records will be created with incorrect dates and times. This might go on for weeks before being noticed and will require lots of work to fix, if it's possible at all.

FYI

If you are connected to a hosted file, you can use Get(CurrentHostTimestamp) to get the current date and time from the server, not the local user.

Repeating Fields

These are *very* useful, and at the same time, a huge bear trap for the FMP newcomer. The rule is simple:

DON'T USE THEM!

Why not?

Repeating fields become a serious problem when data in them has to be altered, manipulated, retrieved, used in calculations, reported on, exported or imported. You will create severely difficult programming conundrums for yourself if you use them outside of the parameters described as follows…

Repeating fields are a holdover from the earliest versions of FileMaker. The reason they still exist is that developers have found them very useful for purposes *other* than those originally intended. So not only has FMI kept them; they've actually improved them. This is a tremendous relief for developers who have been wondering if repeating fields would eventually disappear, nullifying much of their past work.

DO NOT use repeating fields to store data the end-user can access or manipulate: addresses, telephone numbers, invoice data, inventory items, etc. In other words, if the user can add to it or change it, directly or indirectly, it should not be in a repeating field.

DO use repeating fields to store developer resources such as graphics, label text, settings, etc.: Things you use to build your interface and control system. This is not to say that repeating fields should always be used for such purposes, but these uses are common. Usually, repeating fields are also global fields.

There are exceptions to the above rules, but they are rare and most definitely reserved for advanced programmers only. If you do not know exactly why you are using a repeating field and why it is a better choice than a standard field, then chances are 99.99% you are using it incorrectly.

Unstored Calculation Fields

Be very, very careful when deciding whether to set a calculation field to *stored*, or *unstored*. If in doubt, set it to stored.

Setting a calculation field to unstored can have some useful advantages, but it can also cause real performance headaches. Unstored calculation fields can make the task completely impossible if your client ever requests that you export all their records to a text file.

Unstored calculations can become a problem when you are viewing a large number of records. If your end-users can potentially view hundreds or thousands of records in a list, all those unstored calc fields must be recalculated on the fly. If you have a number of unstored calcs in each record, this can take a significant amount of time, particularly if some of your unstored calcs depend on other unstored calcs to complete their tasks. I once had an export routine grind away for over 24 hours and never complete its task. There were a half-million records and dozens of unstored calcs in each. The table involved was never meant to be viewed directly or exported to a text file. It worked just fine within its design parameters, which required that only a few records be accessible at one time, but not when the client threw me this curve.

On the flip-side, you certainly do not want to store a calculation, if it references a Get function that is likely to change. For example, a calculation that references the Get (CurrentDate) function changes every day. Storing that calculation will result in it not being refreshed on a daily basis.

Remember, unstored calculations will only calculate when they are needed for display or print purposes. This forces any Get functions to be re-evaluated at the time of the calculation; so this can be very useful.

If a calculation field may need to show a different result depending on the circumstances under which you are viewing it, set it to unstored. Otherwise, set it to stored.

Also, if your field is used as a foreign key field, it must be stored because foreign key fields have to be indexed, and they cannot be indexed unless stored.

As a general rule, if you don't know exactly why a calc field must be set to unstored, set it to stored. You can always change it later.

Lookup Fields

Lookup fields are a necessary part of most any solution. They are needed to archive data that must remain static while at the same time the original data from which the lookup was drawn remains fluid.

In plain English, a lookup field is essentially a one-time copy and paste of data from one location to a second location. Because it's a one-time lookup, it does not regularly refresh itself unless you explicitly command it to do so.

For example, an invoicing system must be able to draw data from a products table. That products table needs to remain fluid (available products and prices change over time). A lookup field (i.e., similar to a copy and paste) in a line items table, looks up the current price and other information from the products table to create a line item for an invoice. Once that line item is created, it must never change! A completed invoice is something that should be "locked in stone." That product was sold at a specific price and must always show that price on the invoice whenever the invoice is referenced in the future, regardless of how product details may change in the products table at a later date. Hence the need for a separate line items table and the use of lookup fields that create permanent records drawn from non-permanent information.

You will sometimes need lookups for other purposes, where some of that data within the record will remain permanent while others may change. If you have a lookup field that is not a simple line item style lookup as described above, make sure it will contain the needed information under all circumstances. Script a re-lookup for those conditions that require it.

This kind of problem often rears its head when a user discovers a mistake in a previously created record and fixes it. If your lookup field(s) depend on that record data, it may need to refresh itself but it won't, because the key fields (those that automatically trigger a re-lookup) for the lookup's relationship will not have changed.

To re-emphasize, lookups only trigger when the key fields that they depend upon are updated in the database.

Test all circumstances that could or should affect a lookup field and make sure you're covered. Also be careful not to perform a re-lookup for an entire data set when only a subset of records needs to be updated (and vice versa). You may inadvertently trade one record with incorrect data for a thousand.

Field Validation

Here's a field-related tool that should simply never be used. The field definition dialog box allows you to set validation rules for a field. Don't do it! Ever!!

Remember the scene in Dead Poets Society where Robin Williams tears pages he dislikes out of a textbook? Tear this page out of your FileMaker book.

If you set validation rules for a field and the user violates those rules, what happens?

He gets a dialog box he doesn't understand and doesn't know what to do about. He also gets irritated with you because his database is locked up tight and he doesn't know why. A good programmer makes certain this sort of thing never happens. I cannot recall a single reason in nearly 20 years of FMP hacking where I needed this feature or even thought momentarily that it might be a good idea.

The modern standard is to use a script trigger upon field exit to evaluate the field via a script that you completely control. If the validation fails then you can choose to automatically fix the data or provide the user with an intelligent dialog to inform them of their mistake.

I once saw a solution in which there were about a dozen or so fields on one layout, all set to the validation that they must contain data. Users who wanted to interrupt their work to go perform a quick task in another section of the database had to go through all twelve dialogs before being allowed to leave the layout they were on!

VIDEO TIP - 17 PLATFORM VIDEO COURSE
Watch the Modern Field Validation video "0984 - Script Triggers - Field Validations".

VIDEO TIP - 17 PLATFORM VIDEO COURSE
Watch the Old School Field Validation video "0527 - Field Validation Option".

When designing a database, make certain you take into account what a user might want/need to go do before a task is complete. Then make certain he can do it, if at all possible. Don't make him a slave to an endless string of data validation dialogs.

And whatever you do, don't set validation rules for an auto-enter field that is set to *Prohibit modification of value during data entry*. If your user can't modify it, why would you need to validate the data in it? (Yes, I've seen this one too.)

Hidden Utility Fields

There are a dozen reasons for these little jewels. It's pointless to list them all. You only need to know it can be done and how to do it. You'll know when you need one.

In the old days, hidden utility fields were often little tiny fields that people would hide on the layout, typically in the upper left corner set to a size of one pixel by one pixel.

In modern versions of FileMaker, hidden utility fields are designed to be placed on the right side of a layout, beyond the defined edge of the layout. Fields that are in this area will not be directly accessible by the user but can be available by a script that the user may run. Keep in mind that fields in the non-viewable area on the right side will not be in the tab order.

There will most likely be some minimal performance penalty because of this. Keep in mind if a field is drawn visible for a user, it requires FileMaker to render and process that field. A completely hidden field typically will not consume any processing time, other than to load the hidden data into memory. The hidden field on the side of a layout splits the difference in performance with more than zero impact, but less than a fully viewed field that might be on the layout.

One of the more modern uses for hiding fields on the side of the layout is for sorting and exporting processes. FileMaker will frequently give you the option to sort or export just the fields that are in a layout. This option allows you to have fields that are easily included in a sort or export order, while not being visible to the user.

Of course, there are many, many other practical reasons to hide fields on the side of the layout. You will discover these as time goes on.

Field Conventions

There are a number of naming conventions in circulation for fields, scripts, etc. Some developers do not pay attention to naming conventions at all, while others will practice an almost obsessive-compulsive disorder (OCD) level of naming conventions.

To help train new users how to organize relationships and structure naming conventions, we have developed a naming convention document that is separate. We also have several videos that talk about naming conventions.

I would stick with these naming conventions until you become "senior" enough to argue the pros and cons of different techniques. If you have enough experience to debate the technical pros and cons of different naming conventions, then you are probably past the point of needing to read this book.

It doesn't matter how clever someone else's naming convention is if you are not comfortable with it. After all, the person who will most likely need to make sense of your code at a later date is you. However, try to avoid cryptic schemes. They may seem clever, but you will come to regret their use.

No matter how tempting, never, ever use spaces in your field names. Punctuation is out too. The only exception to this rule is the underscore character "_" and vertical pipes "|".

If and when you put your databases on the web, you will find your work is much more difficult if you have spaces or punctuation in your field names.

Plugins also sometimes reject the presence of these characters in field names, forcing you either to change the names, or do a lot of extra, unnecessary coding. There is no benefit to using spaces or punctuation, so why do it? Field names are just as easily understood, and sometimes more easily, if named like one of these examples:

- *myField*
- *my_Field*
- *My_Field*
- *myField_One*

I sometimes prefer to reserve the underscore character to differentiate a subgroup or finer delineation of fields, such as:

- *Contacts_FirstName*
- *Contacts_LastName*
- *Staff_FirstName*

VIDEO TIP - 17 PLATFORM VIDEO COURSE

Watch one of our Naming Convention videos "1131 - Anchor Buoy Design Methodology Part 2".

Download a PDF on Naming Conventions:

http://bit.ly/FMNamingConventions17

- *Staff_LastName*
- *Housekeeping_RecordCrumpler*
- *g_recordcount*

Pick whatever approach you like best, and stick to it.

The same advice given above applies to value lists, table names, file names, table occurrence names, custom functions, etc. Just get into the habit of using only letters and the underscore character to name everything, and you will run no risk of creating unnecessary work and problems for yourself.

Field Name Pairs For Relationships

I said that your field naming convention should be what you're comfortable with, as long as it follows certain basic rules. However, if you start the names of fields with a lower case letter, you might wish to reconsider; changing your field naming convention to *FieldName* instead of *fieldName*.

The reason for this is that some fields, such as globals, can provide additional benefit from having names that indicate what type of field they are.

For example, *gFieldName* makes it immediately apparent that this is a global field. This is helpful when you want or need the fields on both sides of a relationship to have the same name; primary key = *gFieldName*, foreign key = *FieldName*. It is immediately obvious which field is on which side of the relationship, and that they are in fact a "pair" of key fields. With few exceptions, the fields on both sides of a relationship should be similarly or identically named. Otherwise you can end up with key pairs that look like *FieldName* and *TheCreatureFromMars*. Weeks or maybe only days down the road, you won't recognize that these two fields are a pair.

If your naming convention produces *gfieldName*, it will be much more difficult to pick out at a glance than *gFieldName* or *g_FieldName*.

You'll find you use a lot of global fields as primary keys for all sorts of purposes, so the above approach will help a lot.

> **FYI**
>
> Some consulting companies are very OCD about using this process as well. At my company, we limit the use of this to global fields only - not all the other kinds of fields that a developer may want to notate.

Naming Scripts

When naming fields, FMP will warn you if you are using a character it doesn't like, but there are no such warnings in the Script Workspace.

FMP will allow you to name a script anything you like, with any characters at all... Don't do it!

Sooner or later you will run into problems similar to those created by improperly named fields. Follow strict rules in the Script Workspace also. After all, it is easier to follow one set of rules everywhere, than a different set in each area.

I recommend that you number the scripts and group them in a way that makes sense to you. In FM Starting Point we group all of the Contacts scripts, and all of the Invoices scripts, etc. We number the scripts, so when we are trying to identify a specific script, we can reference it by a four-digit number. These groupings become handy because you will run into other developers who will have a script that they called "Print Label." Frequently they will have four or five scripts in the same file, named "Print Label," with each script completing the task differently. Doing this is a total disaster for ongoing support of a FileMaker customer. So feel free to group the scripts into folders and number the various groups.

Keep in mind that as you build new scripts, expect that numbers will go out of order. Periodically during your development process - maybe when you are shipping a new version to a customer - you will want to go through the Script Workspace and "resequence" all of the numbers into some coherent order.

We frequently like to have our brand new Junior FileMaker Developers do this as part of their learning process.

There are three main areas where you will run into sensitivity with script naming.

1) Anytime you are activating scripts from the web publishing engine (i.e., you are accessing it from PHP or the FileMaker DATA API on FileMaker Server). Calling a script from PHP of other web processes wil always require an explicit name and should be considered "fragile."

2) Another area you run into sensitivity is if you're trying to activate FileMaker scripts by calling an external URL protocol. Doing this is a decidedly more advanced skill set. But imagine if you have a web viewer and you press a button on the web viewer, that web viewer may activate a script in the same FileMaker file that you are in currently. Creating a non-web compatible script name is a bad idea. In this case, spaces and other funky characters will be a hassle.

3) The last area of script naming is if you have other scripts in the solution that call this script by an explicit name. Calling objects by an explicit name should be avoided. In most cases, this can be avoided

if you're within a FileMaker solution. Remember, FileMaker has hidden internal ID fields help to identify fields, scripts, and layouts, even if those items have their names changed. If you call a script by an explicit name, then you're bypassing FileMaker's automatic hidden ID number for tracking.

Cut & Paste Will Ruin Your Data

You need two things for a database: *users and data*. The data will behave itself. The users won't. Whatever they can do to ruin your data integrity, they will most certainly do with haste.

One of the things you cannot avoid is cut and paste. While inputting data, end-users absolutely will cut data out of other files and paste it into FMP fields. They will paste italic text, bold text, underlined text, every font and font size but the one you programmed into the database and a myriad of things you can't even imagine. Then, if they notice what they've done at all, they will simply shrug their shoulders and say, *Oh well!*

You cannot let this happen, so...

For every single field to which end-users have access and into which it is possible to paste anything that isn't a graphic, you need a data entry calc that removes all formatting from the pasted text. This way, as soon as the user tabs out of the field into which he has just entered last week's garbage, FMP will immediately remove it all, leaving just nice clean unadulterated data.

In the field definitions area of *Manage Database*, under *Options for Field "YourFieldName"* set the Calc definition under *Calculated Value* to:

TextFormatRemove (Self)

Be sure to uncheck *Do not replace existing value of field (if any)*.

This by the way, is the very best argument I know for creating new fields only by duplicating existing fields and then altering them. That way you don't have to re-enter this calc for every single field and you are far less likely to forget such a vital feature.

Where to Put Graphics Globals

I've already discussed storing graphics in global fields. The nice thing about global fields in modern versions of FileMaker is that they are accessible from anywhere in a solution, without the necessity of a relationship, and regardless of what table contains them or what table you are currently engaging. So put all your graphics-containing global fields in one place. Put them either in the preferences table, or a dedicated table for this purpose. When it comes time to upgrade your solution to a newer version, or prepare a solution for distribution, you'll be very glad you did this.

Variables

Modern versions of FileMaker, now have variables added. Previously, we would define fields explicitly for temporarily storing data that we needed in a script. Now, with the advent of variables, data that we don't want to save in the database, but that we need to track for scripting purposes, should be managed with variables. If you have not gotten heavily into scripting yet, then just make a note for when you do want to track data temporarily within a script, or between scripts. You'll want to use variables and not define extra fields in your solution for that purpose.

Example of Global Variable: $$id_current_user

Example of Local Variable: $script_parameter

Global Variables

For novices and less experienced developers, I recommend just using global variables - these are variables which start with the name of $$. As you can probably guess, global variables are almost like global fields in that; they aren't shared between users. When you open a FileMaker solution, either locally or from the server, no global (or local) variables come pre-defined. Only as you explicitly define global variables within your scripts will they begin to collect in memory.

As a general rule, we have never seen performance problems with defining global variables and leaving them defined while your user is using the database. However, on a personal note, I typically have less than 50 variables defined at any given time within one of our solutions.

Global variables are mentally easier to wrap your head around because they work just like global fields, except they always start off blank. Global variables are specific to a FileMaker file and are not shared between multiple FileMaker files, the same as global fields. Closing a FileMaker file will result in all of the values in the global variables being dumped from memory. Global variables are never saved.

Local Variables

Local variables are similar to global variables, except that they only live during the execution of the script that defined them. In simple terms, you define them in a script, and when that script ends, FileMaker automatically dumps them from memory and blows them out. It may present some challenges to newer FileMaker users who expect the variables to act like global fields (as they do in the previous section). However, more advanced developers sometimes like to define variables for a one-time temporary scripted process. So when the script ends, the developer is happy that these variables get dumped. The main upside to using a local variable is that you don't have to worry about these things collecting and accidentally using a variable that was previously defined elsewhere.

Monitoring Variables

It is easy to monitor variables by using the Data Viewer in FileMaker Pro Advanced. At any given time, the Data Viewer will show you all of the global variables that it can find in memory. Of course, you will notice that local variables will only be visible when a script is running. This only happens when you pause a script using the Script Debugger. Once the script is complete, the local variables are terminated from memory and will be removed from the Data Viewer as well.

2 Layouts

Angry Fruit Salad

I learned this term years ago, and still get a laugh out of it today. It is at once, appropriately descriptive and somehow subliminally naughty.

If your layout has more than two colors on it, and especially if those are bold colors, you have a case of *Angry Fruit Salad*. In other words, do not make your layouts look like Christmas trees. And especially, don't make your layouts look like several different Christmas trees!

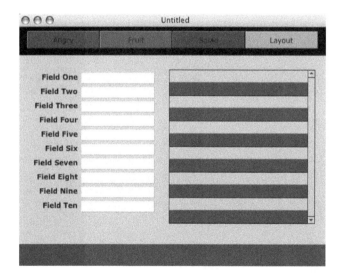

Pick two, and only two colors for use on all of your layouts. Make them severely muted colors, not bold, and make them complementary. Do not use bright red for example, or forest green. Take a look at the other software on your hard drive; the professionally built products. Study them carefully. In most of them you will see that there is one primary color and one secondary color, both soft and non-combative, and that is all! There will be variations in saturation of these colors, but nothing more. If you need contrast, don't pick another color. Use the same color you already have and just lighten or darken it.

FYI
To better assist you in building a clean user interface, feel free to start with a clean copy of FM Starting Point **OR** one of the several user interface example files, that are available at the FMSP Marketplace: http://bit.ly/FMSPmarket17

Another Angry Fruit Salad symptom is different backgrounds for different layouts. The result is a very confusing user experience. You cannot expect a user to switch from one layout to another, see a completely different theme, and not be confused.

Design your layout background and color scheme, and use them exactly the same way on every single layout the user will see because, the user's impression should be that he is on the *same layout all the time*. Just the fields and indicators change, nothing else.

Think of it in terms of a book or magazine. There are common elements that repeat themselves on every page. If one page were white, one green and the next yellow, with the logo in a different position on every page, readers would quickly become confused and annoyed.

Layout Size Consistency

This topic is really very simple...

Concrete rule prior to 2010: all your layouts must be the exact same size without exception, without a single pixel of difference anywhere, and your users must never, ever see a scroll bar anywhere, except in a portal or scrolling text field. A database is not a web browser or a text editor. Scroll bars are strictly verboten. Why?

When you are working with a customer, testing a new FileMaker solution, the following can be problematic: objects that will be hidden or otherwise not visible to the user, critical items that are buried in popover windows or items at the bottom of a layout, which must be scrolled to.

I would strongly recommend that the need to scroll be very apparent to the user and that critical data or interface elements not be buried in hidden locations.

Since 2010, we have been developing FileMaker solutions for mobile devices. Scrolling on a mobile device is a more accepted practice. I would still work hard to avoid this practice on a desktop or laptop computer.

Object Jumping - "Pixel Shift"

*Object ju*mping or pixel shift is something that invariably accompanies Angry Fruit Salad. I have caught many so-called professional developers making this mistake.

Any object that appears on multiple layouts must occupy exactly the same position, to the pixel, on each and every layout. If you have two layouts containing the same field or button for example, and that object is one pixel to the right on one layout as compared to the other, when switching between layouts the object will appear to jump or "shift". This may seem minor, but it is not.

Fix it. You must retain the illusion that these are static objects, all on the same layout. And in fact, you may at times even have to add otherwise unnecessary graphic elements to your layouts, just to retain and reinforce this single-layout illusion.

One way to minimize having to constantly fix object jumping is to create new layouts by duplicating existing layouts (sound familiar?). This way you know your background objects and other common elements are sure to be in the same position from layout to layout.

OPINION

Before you ship a new version of a database to a customer, make sure you follow your "launch checklist". The launch checklist should include the task of checking for pixel shift in the layouts. Download our FMSP Launch checklist here:

http://bit.ly/FMSPLaunchChecklist17

Fonts

On your layouts, use one font only. Instead of using fonts to differentiate the kind of information that you want to convey to the people, you should use a color scheme that varies. Limit the color scheme to no more than three levels of grey and two or three accent colors, to prevent what we call the Christmas tree effect.

You can use a light grey for field labels, black for the fields themselves, and a standard grey for disabled or non-editable fields. If you want to emphasize the field is non-editable, do not put a border around it.

OPINION

This Font section has been written by UI design expert Nick Hunter (see About the Authors page).

Field Label Colors

Make the text color of the labels for your fields considerably lighter than the text color in the fields themselves. You do not want labels visually competing with field content.

Bold, Underline, Extend, Condensed, etc.

Use FileMaker styles sparingly. If you use a FileMaker style only when needed, it will help draw attention to that block of text on the layout. If you overuse the styles, then everything will appear to be special. Therefore, the user's eye will not be drawn to any one spot. Doing this also contributes to the angry fruit salad issue.

Data Text vs Everything Else

Don't use any fields, lines, boxes or other graphic objects with dark colored borders. Mute border colors significantly. The only dark color you want on your layouts is the data in fields, and possibly the background, though the latter is usually a bad idea (it takes a real professional designer to pull this off). Light surroundings lead the eye to the darker text/data which is the point of a database. Dark surroundings compete and make the viewer strain his eyes trying to pick out the data from the clutter.

Visually Indicate Unuseable Items

Make sure that any fields or buttons the user cannot get into or use, are grayed-out, with a noticeably lighter text color, or better yet (in some cases), make them invisible. If an inaccessible field looks the same as an accessible field or if a visible and seemingly useable button mysteriously does nothing, the user will be confused and then annoyed.

(See Chapter 9 – *Techniques*.)

Field Elbow Room

Set the paragraph attribute of your fields (*Inspector-Appearance-Paragraph-Indents*) to indent 3 to 5 pixels on both the left and the right. This is very subtle but makes a huge difference in how your fields look and feel. It works on any kind of field, not just text.

Grouping Like Data

Separating groups of data on the same layout into visible sections (only two or three at the most, per layout). To create a section, make a box, set it to embossed or engraved, set the fill color to slightly darker or lighter than the background. Make sure the border is not dark.

This section tells the user that the data in the section is grouped and somehow distinct from the data placed directly on the background or on another platform, etc.

We have a really good User Interface Design Course available at http://learningfilemaker.com/ui.html that is part of a bundle. In that course, we cover this topic in great detail.

FYI

The User Interface Design Course is part of The Complete Learning FileMaker Subscription Annual Software and Training Bundle.

This bundle includes a FULL copy of FileMaker Pro, over 70 hours of video training, PLUS exclusive video content!

http://bit.ly/LFSubscribe17

Familiar Object Locations

All good software is designed with a specific strategy for the location of particular classes of items. Navigation tabs at the top and/or one side of layouts, record searching/selection tools along the left or less often, the right side, and data manipulation/creation buttons at the bottom of the layout. These locations are where your users expect to find these things. Don't disappoint them. If in doubt, look at some professionally designed software that has things located exactly where you are accustomed by experience to look for them in all software. (Imagine if the back button were in a different location in every web browser!)

Get Your Client's Logo Immediately

This is often overlooked and can cause you a tremendous amount of extra work. Your client has a logo. If they do not, don't start designing your layouts until they have one.

Your client's logo will have a color theme and the layout colors you choose for your project must blend well with that theme. Make your layouts more muted than the logo. The client will want their logo on all of the layouts. If they say they do not, count on them changing their mind later.

Make certain you have at least two, possibly more versions of the logo. You need low resolution (96 ppi) color for your FMP layouts and for possible web use. You also need both high definition color and high definition B&W for printing reports and other likely uses.

Get the logo now. Imagine building 100 layouts only to discover that your layout colors clash horribly with the client's logo. 'Nuff said?

Flashing

Sometimes, when you change record selection within a layout or perform other tasks, certain items on the layout will flash. That is, they will blink in and out of view. This is unacceptable and can have several causes. It is usually easy to fix, but fix it regardless. Professional software does not flash, ever.

First, make liberal use of the Freeze Window script step. Use it at the beginning of all your scripts. It can't hurt anything and will save you a lot of bug hunting later.

Flashing is sometimes caused by another object overlying or underlying the edge of the layout object that is flashing. Move the flashing object around to see if that stops it. Just remember, you cannot allow object jumping in order to get rid of flashing.

Another technique for minimizing flashing is to pop open a new window and relocate it offscreen at the beginning of your script. This is a cool trick and somewhat counterintuitive.

Despite what you might think, the monitor of the computer is much larger than the shiny glass display in front of your face. The very top left corner of the screen is position 0,0. However, if you go -3000,-3000 you are talking about a position that is probably a number of inches above and to the left of your current monitor. It is invisible to you, but the computer can still see it. Very cool!

If you locate a window there and it does a lot of flashing, you can rest assured that the user will not see it. As a side note, at the end of your script, you will need to bring that window back to visible, close the window, or othewise account for it. If you pop open a window there and the script ends, that window will stay there and hang out until a script closes it or the user quits FileMaker.

Always Have an About Screen

Every professionally built software solution has an "About" screen. It looks professional, provides information to the user about what the software is, who owns it, who designed it, what version it is, etc. You can also list your contact info if you think it is necessary. This screen should be accessible from a button on the Main Menu. This script should take the user to the "About" screen that is paused indefinitely, so the user can see the information whenever they wish. It should not smash itself on the user's screen every time someone opens the database (splash screen).

Startup Scripts

Regardless of the complexity of your solution, you absolutely will need a script(s) to run on startup. You don't want your user watching all of the jumping around and goings on while your solution readies itself for use. If the Startup script takes a long time to run, you may want to have an intermediate screen that says "Database Loading" or "Startup script is in progress." Your Startup script can immediately display this message and then freeze the window so that the user cannot see that anything else is happening.

Keep in mind, in these modern days, people expect the software to spin up and be instantly available. Minimizing the overall duration of the startup script is ideal. If your startup script starts to take more than 10-15 seconds to run, then you need to look at off-loading that work onto a FileMaker robot.

TERMINOLOGY

A "FileMaker Robot" is a dedicated FileMaker client machine (ie: Mac or Windows computer.) This machine runs a script on some sort of pre-established schedule to pre-calculate and save values that users will likely need at a later time. A Robot is its own dedicated hardware and is not shared with any other task.

Determine Window Size Before Creating Layouts

This one can cause you an unbelievable amount of unnecessary work, and it is so simple to avoid.

Novices invariably start a project without thinking about window size. They usually just use the size FileMaker presents to them when a new file is created. This can result in having to redesign every single layout when the project is presumably done.

At one time this was less of a sticking point because most computers had 15 inch monitors and all had pretty much the same resolution. Today, things are different. Monitors come in a variety of sizes and offer many different resolution settings. You will especially run into this difficulty if the monitor on which you are developing the project is substantially different in size and/or resolution from the monitors your client will use.

Do not pick a window size for your project at random. Find out what monitors and resolution options your client has and is likely to have in the future. Make a mock-up database file with a few layouts of different sizes and check them to see how they look on the different monitors on which they will be displayed. Make sure there is some text and graphics on the layout.

Don't forget about laptops. When a window size turns out to be too large, it is usually a laptop that is the culprit and more often than not, a Windows laptop. Some Windows users will have visible bars at the bottom of their screens that others do not. Don't assume Mac users don't have similar issues. Take all possibilities into account.

Not much will make you look worse than the CEO of the company having to scroll your database window on his laptop every time he wants to see all of a layout! (Remember, never make a user scroll to see anything, unless and only if, he is scrolling up and down in a report generated in a temporary, secondary window, never in your main window.)

Select a window size that will look best on the smallest, lowest resolution screen that will be used. Adjust the window size of your mock-up until it fills the screen exactly. (Make sure if you are showing or hiding the Status Toolbar then account for that space as well.) Then see how that window looks on the other machines.

Some adjustments may have to be made to the resolution or types of monitor the client is using. You certainly don't want to select a window size that looks good on an old low-resolution 17-inch LCD monitor. It will look terrible on everything else. Don't be shy about telling the client he needs a new monitor.

You will run into employees who are stubborn about changing the resolution of their monitors. Theirs may be the only machine that does not display your solution correctly. You may have to add steps in your startup script that check for monitor resolution and adjust layout magnification accordingly. This often results in less-than-optimally displayed fonts and graphics, but compromises may have to be made.

Once you have selected an optimal window size for your solution, remember that every layout in your solution must be precisely the same size, to the pixel. Otherwise, you will have scroll buttons popping in and out of existence, and layout parts jumping all over. Every square millimeter of every layout must be adequately available to every user on every machine, all of the time, without having to move or scroll windows.

Stay Off the Button and Graphic Bandwagon

One of the first things FileMaker newcomers will find once they start searching the internet for FileMaker related web sites is a plethora of buttons, graphics and layout schemes and themes available either free or for a nominal fee (some, not nominal).

With modern versions of FileMaker, Layout Mode has a built-in icon library based upon "SVG" type graphics. These graphics are very lightweight in nature and can be useful for indicating to your user what a button does. You will most likely find icons you need are missing. You can add additional SVG graphics to your FileMaker library. I recommend visiting www.icons8.com and other SVG free libraries to gather the additional artwork that you need.

FileMaker Pro can accept PNG graphics, but you should stay away from these, they are much slower and harder to process than SVG graphics. You can copy and paste artwork from almost any source into a FileMaker layout.

It is extremely easy to get carried away with using PNG or JPG-type artwork. This will result in creating a layout that is too top-heavy (i.e., it takes a lot of bandwidth for FileMaker to transmit the artwork across the internet).

Remember that your database is about the data it contains, and not about the graphics used to build your layouts. If the user's attention is drawn to the graphics and away from the data, you have used too much eye candy.

The graphics used to build your layouts should draw the user's attention directly to the data and the tools used to manipulate that data, not to the graphic scheme itself. Save the wow graphics for your "About" screen and tone it down by 99% for the rest of your layouts. And remember, big splashy graphics not only detract from the data but as the file is rendered by a user across the internet it takes up a lot of internet bandwidth.

Icons in particular are very popular, and huge wasters of screen real estate (unless they are SVG). Don't use them unless you have a compelling reason. They are more often sources of confusion rather than help. If you can't look at an icon and immediately know exactly what it is for, without needing a tool tip, don't use it. After all, if you need a tool tip, then exactly what purpose does the icon serve?

Finding Waldo (Overstuffing Layouts)

If this title doesn't make any sense, you are too young (or perhaps too old) and should be doing something else, rather than reading all this dry, boring database stuff.

Waldo was (is) a very popular series of children's books that consist of highly detailed and complex drawings in which the goal is to locate a character named Waldo in a sea of other characters and complex background details. (It's kind of like throwing a gross of paper clips on the floor and then asking you to find the bent one.) If you find Waldo in the picture, you win! OK, maybe not too exciting, but kids seem to love it.

Your clients may like playing Find Waldo at home with their children, but don't ask them to do it at the office, in your database.

Virtually every FileMaker newcomer goes down this road and a lot of so-called seasoned developers make exactly the same mistake…

Don't cram your layouts with too much data and too many things to look at. If your user can't take one glance at a layout and immediately know where he is, what he's doing and why he's doing it, the layout is probably too crowded. By that I mean, ineffectual. Take a good look at any book or magazine (skip Wired; they break all the rules and the headache you will get from reading it proves my point).

Notice how much of the page is white space, that is, contains nothing? In order for the human brain to be able to easily digest a page, any page, there must be a lot of white space and the rest of the page must be neat, orderly and immediately make sense.

Spend an afternoon at the library reading a good book or three on page design. These folks know what they're talking about. Pay attention to them.

Novices put too much on a layout because they don't know any better (now you do), but the reason more advanced developers do the same thing is laziness, not ignorance.

Keeping layout clutter to a minimum means creating more layouts. Creating more layouts means adding to the navigation system in your solution. This is time consuming and tedious, tempting developers to just cram everything into fewer layouts.

Tough! Create the additional layouts anyway.

Always Return Your User to Where He Left Off

If you found lady's lingerie the last time you got off the elevator at the third floor, you will be very disoriented the next time you get off the same elevator at the same floor, to find yourself in sporting goods.

Be sure to keep track of what layout and record the user was on when they perform an action, so you can return them to that same spot when the action is completed. Nothing will disconcert a user faster, especially if he is accustomed to working in only a subset of your database, than to find himself in unfamiliar territory. His experience should always be the same.

A technique to help make this easy, is to frequently spawn hidden windows. The idea is to spawn a hidden window, then perform the work via the script you need completed. Once that work is done, close the window and return the user to the screen they were on.

Drilling For Oil

If you were around before the invention of the graphic user interface, you remember what using a command line interface was like… drilling for oil. Every time you wanted to get somewhere, you had to drill down to it, then drill back out.

If you were using a database, it was the same thing… drill down to what you needed, then drill back out again. Despite the advantages of a graphic user interface and the option of creating aliases/shortcuts to get to wherever you need to go, some databases are still designed by would-be oil tycoons. They just love to drill.

Well, users don't like to drill. Don't force them to go through layout, after layout, after layout to get where they want to go, and then back again, adding insult to injury. (This is another reason why a properly built tabbed interface should always take a user back to the last layout he was on and the last record he was viewing when he left that section.)

If your users have to do a lot of tedious drilling, then you're not thinking outside the box and you're making them pay for it. Find another way. One way is via popover window objects. A button pops open a small window that lets users quickly enter or alter some small bit of data without having to navigate to some other layout.

With the advent of menu controls, first offered in version 8 of FMP, even more options are available for avoiding drill-down tedium, because a lot of buttons can be eliminated and replaced with menu items attached to shortcut key combinations.

The Custom Menu system in FileMaker sucks, and FMI knows it. However, it has been bad, for so long, that most people have given up on using it. Because of that, no one complains about it, which results in FileMaker thinking that it is okay. Aka, the never-ending circle of suckage.

Don't Use FileMaker's Buttons as Tabs

Over the years, FMI has made significant improvements, allowing developers to build beautiful and efficient interfaces. FileMaker's tab control capabilities, as well as the (very similar) slide controls, are great tools to use in your interface.

One caveat with the tab controls is that you cannot make specific tabs completely invisible (based on a calculation). For new users, this is typically not a problem, but as a developer responding to the needs of a customer, they are likely to run into a situation where a specific tab panel should be invisible. There is no support for this within the FileMaker product. As a result, if you want to make a tab panel disappear, you have to do a workaround, aka a "hack."

The hack for this is to use a button bar at the top of the slide control. Buttons in a button bar can be "hidden by calculation." A button, within a button bar, can be told to make a specific object visible. You can name each tab or slide panel; so you can explicitly trigger individual panels to be visible. Doing this is a total hack, but it works pretty well.

Watch the video listed on the right to learn how to do it.

> **TERMINOLOGY**
> If you see the word "FileMaker", we are referring to the product or the platform.
>
> If you see the word "FMI" we are referring to the hard-working company that makes the awesome product, except for custom menus. LOL.

> **TERMINOLOGY**
> Trying to get around a product limitation requires a workaround, aka a "hack".

> **VIDEO TIP - COACHES CORNER**
> Watch one of our Coaches' Corner videos on this topic here:
> http://bit.ly/FMCoachesCorner717

Be Sparing With Graphics

It is nice that you can put so many different kinds of graphics into FMP solutions for buttons, backgrounds, etc., but be forewarned…

The graphics you build in FMP, using FileMaker's own tools, are stored as mathematical descriptions and are fast and easy to transfer over a network and to draw on screen (similar to the SVG file format).

Any graphics you import, or paste, into an FMP solution are stored as bitmaps. They are larger, much slower to transmit over a network and take longer to draw. If you know your database will be used over a network, use as few imported graphics as you possibly can. One, your client's logo, is ideal. Your solution will be faster and cleaner. This does not mean you can't use any. Just be very stingy.

If your solution is slow over the network, start stripping out non-FileMaker graphics until it speeds up. Faster is always better than prettier.

Rather than clutter your layouts with a lot of memory-sucking custom tab/button graphics, just use the built-in SVG button icon library and add additional SVG icons from a website like www.icons8.com.

Comments

If you are designing a database solution you are most likely doing so for a client. That client may not know anything about color, layout design, etc., but he will most assuredly know, if only on a subconscious level, when he is viewing something that is visually unsettling. If you present your client with an amateur hour of, confusing fields and buttons or tools located where he has never seen them before, he may very well reject your services, even if he can't quite explain to himself why.

TERMINOLOGY
UI = User Interface
UX = User Experience

I have seen major consulting companies fired because the developers are building very juvenile and unprofessional UI's. Some customers are more sensitive to this than others. Please keep in mind, with the modern age of mobile apps; there is a higher level of polish expected from the user interface.

VIDEO TIP
To learn more about UI and UX, check out our FileMaker UI Design Course at

http://learningfilemaker.com/ui.html

Learn the conventions of style, design and placement and stick to them. Always remember that you are trying to build a database, not re-invent how software looks and behaves.

Also, always remember this universal truth of software development... It is much easier for attractive, intuitive, yet poorly designed software to be successful, than it is for good software with a confusing and Angry Fruit Salad interface. I have seen no commercially successful Angry Fruit Salad software. I have seen lots of software with a good interface and terrible underlying code do quite well.

Apple's Human Interface Guidelines

NOTE
Previously, these guidelines were contained in a nice, downloadable PDF.

Since then, apparently someone at Apple has decided that they hate PDFs, so it is now assembled in a group of non-downloadable webpages.

When it comes to proper design of graphic user interfaces, Apple is the undisputed expert. If you wish to learn more, you can take your fill here: https://developer.apple.com/ios/human-interface-guidelines/overview/themes/

Naturally, I can't know how long that URL will be good, but you can always search the internet for Human Interface Guidelines to find the latest version.

3 Database Design

Don't Build a House Without a Blueprint

Novice developers want to get their hands dirty right away. That is understandable. FMP is cool! It is also deceptively simple to use and the temptation to start building something right away is irresistible.

DON'T DO IT!

This is advice almost every novice developer both receives and ignores. And it is what gets them into more trouble than anything else.

A software project is like anything else you construct. It has to be properly designed first or it will not turn out well. (And by *not turn out well*, I really mean *complete and utter useless disaster*.) You wouldn't think of building a house without a plan, why would you consider building something perhaps even more complicated with no plan at all?

Resist the urge to dive right in and instead, take a few days to draw up a careful and detailed plan of exactly what the software will do and more importantly, how it will do it. To the beginner, this seems like a lot of extra time, but it is not. It is a time saver.

Make the plan sufficiently detailed that you can sit down at the computer and follow it precisely as you build your database(s). The first time or two you do this, you will find that your plan does not include many of the things you discover you need. It will also include a number of things that need to be changed. This is normal. As you gain experience, the plans you make will be more accurate and detailed.

While you build your project, and discover shortcomings or errors in your design, update the design. Don't just make changes to the software and forget to change the written design. Keep it current with what you are really building, so that when the project is finished, your written design is an exact description of the project. This way, when you are done you will have much of the project documentation already finished.

The reason most novices avoid designing databases on paper first is that they don't know how to do it. Because FileMaker is superficially so simple, it is much easier and more tempting to start coding right away than to take time to tackle something not nearly as appealing and

> **FYI**
>
> As you spend more and more time building FileMaker solutions, you will start to do the planning process automatically in terms of understanding what tables need to be created and the general kind of workflows that the user will need.

perhaps completely foreign. Every growth process has its painful stage and this is it. You have to go through it or you won't get where you want to go.

Fortunately, there are a number of books available on software design and one of these will almost certainly help you get started. Also, do a Google search on the phrase *software project plan*. This will provide lots of interesting and helpful information. Reading other people's plans can be quite useful. In the mean time, here are some initial guidelines to follow:

Create a Requirements Analysis document. This is simply a detailed description of what the client needs the software to do, and under what circumstances. This is more difficult than it may appear, because the client usually does not know what he needs. You must help him discover his needs. This can be a problem because clients who are willing to invest their money are often surprisingly unwilling to invest their time. It can also be difficult to make a client realize you cannot gain an understanding of his needs by osmosis and must ask a lot of questions and see his business in action.

Create a Use Case Analysis document. This is a description of exactly how the software will be used by each job category that will need to access it. For example, the sales department will need to see and do things completely different from the accounting department. You will have to know exactly what each user needs to see and how they will need to interact with the software. You cannot begin building your layout and navigation structure, until you know what each person (job description) must be able to do. This will also help you set up security for the software.

Some designers will call this "documenting the customer workflow." Workflow is just as it sounds - a specific process that a customer will follow to accomplish specific tasks within their organization.

Build a detailed Entity Relationship (ER) diagram. (Search the web for examples of all of these documents.) An ER diagram is a representation of your tables and the relationships between them. This is actually not hard to do if you have already done the first two items above.

A more useful description of an ER diagram is that of a map of the real-world objects with which you will be dealing, and the connections between them. In fact, it is very helpful indeed to think in terms of object-oriented programming when designing and building your database(s) even though FileMaker is not an object-oriented programming environment. (A quick tour of an object-oriented programming primer should prove very informative.) Think in terms of each table in your database representing a real-world object. Contacts are real objects. Inventory items are also real objects, as are invoices, line items in invoices, meetings, addresses, phone numbers, etc.

VIDEO TIP - COACHES CORNER

Learn about Directed Workflow in one of our Coaches Corner videos:

http://bit.ly/CoachesCorner1017

VIDEO TIP - 17 PLATFORM VIDEO COURSE

Learn more about FileMaker Relationships in video "0315 - What is a Relationship".

And each object can own other objects. Contacts can own several addresses and invoices can own a line item for that invoice, but an invoice cannot own an inventory item. A meeting object can own a time slot in your calendar, several attendees (contacts), a lecturer (another contact), and an hour in a specified meeting room (but not the meeting room itself; a meeting room is an object which owns its time slots), etc. See how easy this is when you approach it from this perspective?

In object-oriented programming, each object has attributes (a contact has a last name) and functions (things it can do with or to the attributes it contains, like calculating a total for a line item in an invoice). This aspect of the object-oriented perspective is also helpful when thinking about designing a solution in FileMaker.

If you get into the habit of thinking in object-oriented terms, you will find that designing your solution is easier, faster and more accurate.

IMPORTANT →

Include in your design, complete descriptions of how records will be displayed, searched, reported on, how you will navigate between layouts, in what ways users will have access to what records, etc. How these things are done will alter how you approach the structure of your database. If you don't decide them until later in the project, you will have to alter or redo large amounts of work unnecessarily.

Based on all of the above information, design your layout set(s). When you start your project, build your layout and Navigation system first. This will help in many ways, including forcing you to see flaws in your solution's design.

Design your solution with future requirements and adaptations in mind. Down the road your client may decide he wants added functionality that wasn't mentioned at the beginning. When a client tells you he will never need feature X, you can bet your fee he will later ask for it. For example, a client might tell you he only needs to track one address per contact. Create an address table anyway! If you design your software with this sort of possibility in mind, you will save yourself a lot of headaches.

FileMaker Jedi can use their advanced Jedi senses to look into the future and see the problems that the customer's requests may generate.

As you gain more experience building FileMaker solutions for customers, you will be able to anticipate the areas (or functionality) they need in the software that they have not asked for yet. This is purely a function of your experience and not something that is learned over the weekend.

There is more to designing your database(s) than can be covered here. The important point is that you must have a design and follow it. If you do not, the possibility that you will reach a roadblock that forces you to start over is extremely high. And even if you don't run into a brick wall, it is extremely likely indeed that your database(s) will be far less efficient and useful than they could have been.

Your design documents should be sufficiently detailed and accurate that you can follow them like a set of step-by-step instructions. Your first one or two of course, will be more like Chinese bicycle assembly instructions. But you will improve quickly, and you'll be glad you suffered through.

An Object Lesson

In the previous section I briefly discussed the subject of object-oriented programming. A while ago, one of our video viewers made me realize this subject needed expansion in this manual so...

You cannot adequately design a database without first having a complete object list. As explained, this is a list of the real-world (and conceptual) objects with which your database will have to deal. This is neither a simple task nor a trivial requirement and necessitates quite a lot of thought (and a pile of crumpled legal paper on the floor).

One of the hardest things to do is to learn to distinguish between an object and an attribute of an object. An object, with rare exception, requires its own table. An attribute only requires an additional field. Lets use the person object as an example as it is simple and easy to grasp (it gets much more difficult with other, less obvious object types).

A person is an object. If you are going to create a database of contacts, you are dealing with a person object, and you will require a person (or people, or contact, whatever you wish to call it) table. But the creation of a person table immediately implies the need for additional tables. People have addresses, phone numbers, email addresses, etc. These are *not* attributes of a person. A phone number is a separate object, not an attribute of a person (a person cannot comb his phone number). An attribute of a person would be age, eye color, height, weight, IQ, etc.

These are not static; a person can go on a diet and change his weight, but every person gets one each of these attributes. A phone number or address can be transferred to another person or continue to exist after the original owner no longer exists, and a person can own an unlimited number of these objects. These things are separate objects that can be owned by a person object, but are not attributes of a person object. Therefore, if you have a person object, you need a person table, and by implication, additional tables for phone numbers, addresses, email addresses and anything else a person owns but does not embody that you wish to track in your database. Simple, right?

Unfortunately, it's not quite so simple. Just because an address is an object unto itself and is owned by a person object, doesn't mean that having a separate table for addresses is necessarily the best approach under all circumstances.

If a person object in your solution will always have one and only one address (or two and only two addresses, but now we're skirting the edge a bit), you can treat it as an attribute, even though it isn't, and just add one set of address fields to your people table instead of creating a separate address table. This is perfectly legitimate procedure under the right circumstances. The difficulty lies in determining the right circumstances and this brings us to the big question that 99.99% of novice developers (and a frighteningly large percentage of more advanced developers who ought to know better) never ask themselves.

That question is: *What is your solution about?*

This is not flippant or superficial. It is probably the most important question you must answer before opening a shiny new FMP file and adding that first new field. Get this question wrong, or fail to answer it at all, and you will quickly find yourself coded into a corner with no exit. There's nothing more humiliating than having to start a project over from scratch because you missed a fundamental concept.

Let's take a hypothetical situation where we have two different database projects destined for two different clients. Both solutions have substantial similarities in that they contain tables for people, addresses, telephones, email addresses and notes. In the first solution this list of tables is correct for the type of solution created, in the second it is not.

The first solution is a database of customers and potential customers for a sales force. The database is about the contacts (I'm leading you down the garden path a bit here; you'll see why shortly). Sales people want to know everything they can about their customers, tracking all available addresses, telephone numbers, etc., so that they can reach them on vacation, when they're asleep, in the bathroom, at the cemetery burying grandma...

Such a database would be required to do a lot of reporting, much of which is going to involve searches and sorts of addresses, phone numbers, etc., all of which is simpler and more efficient if these bits of information are contained in separate tables. The solution revolves entirely around customers, the objects possessed by those customers, interactions with those customers and the results of those interactions.

The second solution is a database for planning newspaper delivery routes. Newspapers have to be delivered to a customer and therefore this database also needs a people table and obviously, addresses for those people. But a newspaper can only be delivered to one address, customers will seldom need to be contacted by phone or email, and notes will consist of little more than directives to carriers to stop braining the cat with the Sunday supplement.

This solution is about delivery routes, not contacts, and although it might make sense for addresses to be a separate table to facilitate route planning, phone numbers, email addresses and notes are not central to the main purpose of the database and even people will have a secondary role to addresses and routes. The solution is about delivery routes, not people. Therefore all the information relevant to a person would probably be best contained in a single table. Separate tables for addresses, phones, email addresses and perhaps even notes are just not as central and may actually hinder the functionality of the database.

Once you have determined what your solution is about, it will be easier to create an accurate list of objects with which that database must deal. If you are uncertain whether there should be a separate address object, list it as an object, indented under the person object, so that you know its status as a separate object is temporarily in limbo.

A detailed object list will go a long way toward informing you about what you need to build and why. It may be a huge pain to come up with an adequate list, especially the first few times you do it, but it will be an enormous help not too much further down the road and will contribute significantly toward keeping you out of trouble.

The simple yardstick is: *long list good, short list bad*.

Let's go back to the example of a customer database for a sales force. A list of objects a novice might come up with could look something like this:

- *Customers*
- *Telephones*
- *Addresses*
- *Email Addresses*
- *Notes*

This is a great start, but it will not be adequate. After all, there's not much you can do with just these objects. Assuming your sales force does their job well, they will contact these customers frequently. They can hardly record every contact in the notes table. That would be unmanageable and isn't proper database design anyway. A *Contacts* (meaning *interactions* in this case) object is going to be a must and in fact, may well cause you to reconsider the previous answer to the question, "What is the solution about?" Your database may actually be about the interactions of sales staff with customers, rather than the customers themselves. You will have to decide.

Any time a customer is telephoned, sent an email or written a letter, a contact has taken place. Because the purpose of this database is to assist a sales force, and they can only do their job if they contact potential customers, all three of these communication types must be tracked.

Now we must decide whether or not phone calls, emails and letters are separate objects, or all just different flavors of contacts. This depends on what type of reporting will be required (in software development, you generally code the reporting last, but plan it first). For simplicity, we'll assume all three types of communication are different flavors of the contacts object. This means we'll need a contact type attribute for each *Contacts* record.

In addition to outgoing communications, there are also incoming letters, emails and phone calls, necessitating an incoming/outgoing attribute for the Contacts object.

Sales people save a lot of time and work by using canned material. Generic prepared letters, emails and even telephone scripts. It is much easier to plug a page of boilerplate text into an outgoing letter or email, and then alter it to suit the particular recipient, than to write every single communication from scratch. So we will quite obviously need a Boilerplate object if our database is going to meet the needs of our sales staff.

Assuming we have multiple sales people and they don't all have access to all the customers in the database (customers are usually assigned to, and jealously guarded by sales people) we need a way to assign a customer to a sales person. Oops, our list of objects doesn't include sales people. It also doesn't include any administrative staff; people who will have additional access to the database. We could change the concept of the Customers object to a People object and make customer, sales person and staff member attributes of the People object but this could mean considerable extra coding with regard to keeping the sales staff from seeing each other's records and other personnel data to which they should not have access. So a separate Staff table is almost certainly required.

We now have the following objects:

- *Customers*
- *Telephones*
- *Addresses*
- *Email Addresses*
- *Notes*
- *Contacts*
- *Boilerplates*
- *Sales People*
- *Staff*

Customers do not exist in isolation. They are referred by others, refer others and have associations with others. Salesmen need to know these things, especially if they expect to keep existing customers, because a referral without a thank you is the last referral. Therefore the solution will require both a Referral object and a means of connecting customers to each other via a Group object (for example, grouping all members of the same family together). So we need to add these to our list.

Salesmen are notorious for being forgetful. Any communication to or from a customer implies another communication. If a sales person called a customer who wasn't in, he must remember to try again within a certain time period. If he receives a letter from a customer, he must remember to answer it before the paper turns yellow and crumbles. This strongly implies the need for a *To-Do* object. To-do's must be accomplished (generally) by a certain date and or time, which implies a calendar and the several objects which that immediately suggests. Dealing with customers also means appointments; further justification for a calendar. For the sake of simplicity we'll turn a blind eye to all that a calendar implies in the way of additional objects and just lump them all together into one *Calendar* object.

People who have made a purchase tend to eventually make another purchase. In fact, salesmen generally make much more money from previous customers than from new customers. If you sell cars, you know that people tend to purchase a new car every few years: let's say two. You also know that people are very unlikely to purchase a new car today if they just purchased one last week. You don't want to miss contacting someone who bought his last car two years ago, or risk annoying someone who just bought a car from you on Tuesday. You also don't want to offer the latest two-seater sports car to a guy who always buys pickup trucks. This means you'll need a *Sales* object and a *Products* object. Even if you are going to do all your billing, bookkeeping and inventory control in another software package, reserving this database strictly for information related to making sales, your sales staff will still need to know what they sold, to whom and when, and what they can potentially offer for sale.

Our object list is now as follows:

- *Customers*
- *Telephones*
- *Addresses*
- *Email Addresses*
- *Notes*
- *Contacts*
- *Boilerplates*
- *Staff*
- *Referrals*
- *Groups*
- *To Dos*
- *Calendar (intentionally over-simplified)*
- *Sales*
- *Products*

> **FYI**
>
> If you have been following along with this conversation then you have actually followed the process that we followed to build FM Starting Point.
>
> This is our free and unlocked business solution...aka, CRM (customer relationship management) custom FileMaker application.
>
> Download a free copy here:
>
> http://bit.ly/FMSPdownload17

We could go on considerably longer as this list is by no means complete, but I think this is adequate to make the point. Coming up with an object list is one of the first steps to informed design of your database and requires a lot of thought. You cannot create a complete object list until you know exactly what your solution will and will not be required to do. Once you have this list you are then better prepared to create a list of tables. (Not all objects become tables, but they always remain objects at least in concept.)

Having this list not only helps you to determine what you are going to build, but also how to build it. It is essential.

Reports – Build Them Last, Design Them First

This book talks a lot about the preparation you must do prior to adding that first field to the first table. Lots of documentation, planning and design are required. The initial preparation for a project can be very frustrating. This is absolutely the most difficult thing for novices to do and the reason so many simply throw up their hands and start coding without laying a proper foundation.

It's easy for someone like me to smugly say, *you have to design your solution first.* It is quite another thing for a novice to *do* it, or even know where to start. That question is one of the few in database development that actually has a hardwired, useful answer.

Start at the end!

> **VIDEO TIP - 17 PLATFORM VIDEO COURSE**
>
> To learn more about Reporting, watch section "1300 - Printing & Report Creation".

The one thing all FMP solutions have in common is reports. Your client wants to see reports. He wants to be able to view and print his data from a variety of different perspectives. He may want to see a list of contacts sorted by zip code, another by age and yet another by sex. He may also want to print thousands of mailing labels.

A thorough understanding of all the types and forms of reports your client requires will go a very long way in helping you to determine how to design and build your solution. And, asking your client for a detailed list of all the reports he will want, with all the minute variations, is the best way to get focused input from your clients that you might otherwise not be able to extract at all.

The best way to create a proper plan of action for any project is to first know where you are going and in database development, that means *reports*.

Compile a complete and detailed description of all the reports your solution will be required to produce and refer to it frequently while designing your solution. This will help immensely. Here's an example…

You have a client who wants a people database where he will store contacts, customers, suppliers, etc., a wide variety of different classes of people. He wants to be able to assign each person in this table to one of these categories. But he wants to be able to create his own categories, rather than have them hard-wired into the system, and he wants an unlimited number of categories. He also wants reports that give him a printed list of people sorted by category, or a list of people in randomly selected categories. Finally, he wants to store multiple phone numbers and addresses for each person and to see a phone number and address for each person on the aforementioned reports.

Just this little bit of information tells you a great deal about how your database must be designed and you can see it all from the perspective of reports.

Your first inclination with regard to categories might be to create a hard-wired initial value list with the option for users to edit the list set to *on*. The problem with this is that when users are allowed to edit a hard-wired value list, they can edit any part of the list (or even delete the entire list), including entries that have already been assigned to people previously entered into the database. If someone changes customers to clients, your reports suddenly break because there are now two categories of people (customers and clients) who are really the same. But your client wants to do exactly this. He wants to be able to make this change and yet have reports remain consistent.

A value list drawn from the contents of the field won't work either, because this allows users to create new values for categories simply by inventing one on the spur of the moment or by misspelling one that already exists. Reports break again. In addition, your client will undoubtedly want only authorized personnel to be able to add a new option to the categories value list.

This should make it immediately obvious that you need a separate table to contain this list of values that is accessible only in the administration section of your solution. (It also tells you that you need an administration section.) Each record in this new table must contain a non-modifiable identifier key field and of course a text field to contain the category value. Users must also not be able to delete the text from one of these fields if it has already been assigned to at least one person, and they cannot duplicate an already existing entry.

The categories contained in this table must be assignable to people via their identifier key field rather than the text field, because the text field can be altered at will by the administrator. (The category value list used to assign categories to people can be drawn from the identifier field, but set to show only the text field.) Since categories are assigned to people via the identifier key field, changing the category text in the admin area immediately changes the text that appears in the category field on all people records, and keeps your reports from breaking.

Having solved the problem of administrative changes to the categories list breaking your reports, you now have to face the problem of the phone numbers and addresses required on those reports.

You client has already told you that he wants to track multiple phones and addresses for each person. This implies a separate table for each and immediately causes several problems with regard to reports. Let's further complicate the problem by stating that the client wants multiple phone numbers, addresses and categories (home, office, vacation, etc.) for each phone number and address, for each person. Of course, he only wants to see one address and one phone number in his reports, which raises the question, *which phone number and which address?*

The report previously mentioned was people (their names) sorted by category. Both of these fields are contained in the people table. But phone numbers and addresses are stored in their own separate tables. The rule of thumb when creating a report is to go to the furthest table in the relationship hierarchy. But you have a problem here because there are two furthest tables, phones and addresses. You can't exactly go to both of them, and neither of them contains the name or category fields in the people table, which fields are the primary concern of the report. (You can put them there with lookups, but this brings its own problems with data-integrity control and still doesn't solve the problem of having two tables furthest down the line.)

There are a number of possible solutions to this conundrum, depending on your client's reporting requirements. One possibility is…

Set up your address and phone number tables so that there is a field to mark an address as the primary address or phone for each person. This could be a checkbox in each address and phone number portal with a script attached that un-checks all other rows in the portal and checks the one in question. Checking an address or phone number row as the primary related record puts a 1 (one) into that field (create a hard-wired value list called One that contains only the number 1[one]). A global calc field set to always contain a 1 (one) in the people table establishes the primary key for the relationship. These have to be multi-key relationships or each people record will see all the primary address and phone number records for all people. Now you need to add the primary key and foreign key ID fields to the relationship and you will have established new relationships for primary addresses and phone numbers.

To clarify; in addition to the traditional relationships between your people table and the address and phone tables (primaryKey >> secondaryKey), you'll need another, multi-key relationship for each:

PrimaryKey >> secondaryKey

GlobalCalcField >> primaryAddressMarker (both fields containing a 1 [one])

PrimaryKey >> secondaryKey

GlobalCalcField >> primaryPhoneMarker (both fields containing a 1 [one])

Call these two relationships PrimaryAddress and PrimaryPhone. Now to create your report you only need to select the appropriate records in the people table via traditional means and print from a layout showing people records. This layout will contain the name and category fields from the people records and related fields from the PrimaryAddress and PrimaryPhone relationships.

This is all easy to do and works great if your client only wants reports showing the primary addresses and phone numbers for his people table. But what if he wants reports that can show any combination of address and phone number? What if he wants to see a report that shows home addresses and office phone numbers, or primary addresses and home phone numbers, or office addresses and primary phone numbers?

Remember the discussion about creating a separate table to draw on for the categories field in people? Since your client wants the same category versatility for addresses and phones, you will need to create the same kind of tables there. But remember, we actually populated the category field in people with the ID numbers rather than the text values from the categories table so that when the owner changes the text of a category name it automatically changes the text everywhere else. If we do the same thing for addresses and phones, then the category fields in the addresses and phones tables will actually contain numbers though they display text; ideal for a simple relationship!

Change the global calc field mentioned previously to two global number fields so you can turn the relationships on and off via script by setting the fields to one or zero.

Create two more relationships from people to addresses and phones:

PrimaryKey >> secondaryKey

GlobalAddressCategoryKey >> addressCategory (field contains the category number)

PrimaryKey >> secondaryKey

GlobalPhoneCategoryKey >> phoneCategory (field contains the category number)

On the layout originally designed for the report in question, duplicate the address and phone fields and place them exactly over the top of the original address and phone fields, changing them to the two relationships shown above (be sure the overlaying fields are set to no fill so the fields under them can be seen if they are the fields required).

Now you have overlaying address and phone fields; one set of fields for the original relationships to show primary addresses and phones, and the other for the new relationships that show these items via selected address and phone categories. To make it work, your scripts simply have to put the right numbers into the global fields in the people table.

If you want to see the primary address and the home phone number in the report, put a 1 (one) in the primary address key field, a 0 (zero) in the primary phone key field and a 2 (if the record ID number is 2 for that option in the phone categories table) into the GlobalPhoneCategoryKey field in people. By turning these relationships on and off and changing the number in the GlobalAddressCategoryKey and GlobalPhoneCategoryKey fields you can show any combination in your report.

The point of this section is not the how-to aspect of the foregoing, but rather to demonstrate the fact that the type of report the client required allowed us to determine in advance the proper design for this portion of the database. This is a very simple example involving only one report type.

The detailed list of reports mentioned previously, compiled at the outset of a project, will provide exponentially greater insight into the necessary design for your database.

So if you're stumped with regard to designing your database, before you start coding, or do anything else, enter through the exit. Let your reports show you the way to begin designing your database.

Lock Users Out of Everything

This is a big one. It is one of the most significant traps for the beginning FMP developer, and virtually everyone falls into it. Falling prey to this will cause you many, many extra hours of work and frustration, and very possibly the loss of all your data.

FileMaker can be used to build anything from the simplest single-user (you) database to the most sophisticated multi-user system. It lends itself to use by novice and professional alike. However, none of the literature I have seen explains this vital information to the novice...

If you are building a database for your personal use, and no one else will have access to it, then nothing under this heading applies (sorta). But if even one person aside from yourself will access your database, this may be the most important advice you'll get:

FileMaker is a software development tool, not a pre-built solution.

An analogy: Let's say you need somewhere to live. FileMaker is like Home Depot. It is a place that sells all the tools you need to build your own house. Home Depot itself is not a house. It is just a collection of excellent tools.

If FileMaker is Home Depot, then it is an excellent collection of tools to build your software app. Keep in mind; there are some software building tools in FileMaker which the FileMaker user (someone other than you) must never access.

Say for example, you get an electric saw from Home Depot. You need this saw to cut the boards for your house. You do not, when finished, sit your child down in the house to play with the electric saw. If you are fond of your new house (or the child) you will put your tools away, out of reach. You must do the same with the dangerous tools you use in FileMaker.

The obvious things, like not allowing users to define fields or relationships are easy to understand. But there are some not-so-obvious things too.

The tools to which your end-users must never have access are potentially everything in the menus, and in the status area.

If this shocks you, consider the alternatives...

Most of the items in the FileMaker menus must be made unavailable to the end-user. Allowing a user to simply select New Record from the Records menu can be disastrous if certain housekeeping tasks must be performed before, during or after the creation of a new record (extremely likely). This is often the case, and most of the other options in the normal FileMaker menus must be off-limits for similar reasons.

It is super critical to review your FileMaker solution to determine if the Status Toolbar can be left visible. There are tremendous benefits

IMPORTANT

Our free business software, FM Starting Point (FMSP), ships out completely unlocked. We do this to provide a great training tool for people to learn this material without impeding them by keeping them locked out of areas.

If you are going to actually deploy FMSP to an end customer (which you can do free of charge) then you will probably want to follow the conversation about locking it all down.

VIDEO TIP - 17 PLATFORM VIDEO COURSE

This Home Depot analogy is discussed more in video "0105 - The FileMaker Platform - Summary".

Some of these course videos are also posted to YouTube:

https://youtu.be/6DuHjhvjh1o

to having the status toolbar visible to customers. As I have mentioned elsewhere, we ship FMSP with the status toolbar visible in most sections.

However, as you build a mission-critical application for a customer, ask these questions:

Will you have a controlled process for creating new records?

Will you have a process which uses a script that properly controls the creation of a new record? If so, you need to suppress the status toolbar and create yourself an alternate version, which you have specific controls over.

If you have carefully controlled navigation between layouts using buttons and scripts, then you certainly do not want users to have access to the Layout popup menu in the status toolbar. True, you can set layouts to not show in that menu, but that violates one of the basic rules of software design: don't let the user see something he can't use and for which he doesn't understand the purpose. If you have scripts that navigate between layouts (and you should), then sooner or later

you will also incorporate steps in those scripts that perform vital tasks before leaving the layout or upon arriving at the new layout, making it impossible to permit enduser access to the Layout popup in the status toolbar.

This is also potentially true of the navigation scrollbar in the status area (at the top of your window).

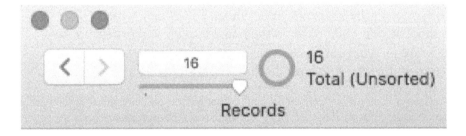

This icon allows users to navigate between records (or layouts) freely, but that scrollbar is there for you, the developer, not your end-user. For your end-users, you want to control navigation with scripts.

There are so many ways an end-user can throw a wrench into your database if he has access to menus or the status area, that this rule really doesn't have any exceptions.

At the end of the day, there are two ways of proceeding.

- Adjust the security privilege sets to lock users out of the menus. This is the most expedient method, but the users can see the menus and the grayed-out selections in those menus, but they can't use them and won't understand why they are there.

OPINION

David and I have conflicting opinions on the Status Toolbar, but fundamentally we agree. If you have mission-critical processes that you have to control, and the status toolbar allows the users to bypass those processes, then you need to remove the toolbar.

However, I try to keep applications as simple as possible and allowing users to have access to the status toolbar is one way to do that. This is also very educational for people who are learning FileMaker.

You may consider creating a solution where some areas have the status toolbar visible and some do not, depending upon the needed controls for a particular section of the application.

For example, in FMSP on the Home screen, we suppress the status toolbar because it is unwise to let users play in that area. However, when they reach the Contacts section, we do not have a scripted process to create new records. So allowing users access to the status toolbar is something that we allow in that section.

- The second method is to build custom menus to completely replace FileMaker's existing menus. Again, FileMaker's implementation of the Custom Menus is convoluted and poorly implemented. So plan on spending some time learning this, if you want to master it.

Excessive Cleverness (everything on one layout with lots of portals and tabs)

This is a very advanced topic. None-the-less, it is one that novices should be aware of before starting a more complex project. Without this knowledge, you may put a great many hours into building a solution that cannot be salvaged.

The crux of the problem is this:

As FileMaker developers get more experienced, they like to try new and different techniques to expand or explore their evolving skill set. Sometimes building a database with a specific technique (just "because you can") is not a good reason. One such design methodology is accessing related data through a very deep relational structure. Consider this scenario:

You are designing a parts database for an auto-parts chain. You will no doubt need a hierarchy of related tables something like this:

Manufacturer -> Year -> Model -> PartsGroup -> Part

Obviously, it would make sense that you would have a Manufacturer, Year, Model, PartGroup, and Parts table. How you interact with these can greatly affect the performance of a FileMaker file.

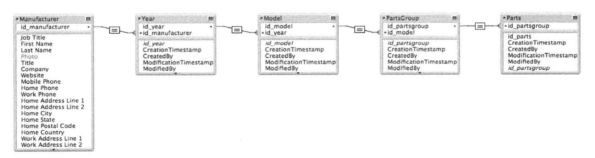

You could build the layout, so the user drills down through a portal to select the Year. Then, the user goes through another portal to select the Model, and another portal to select the PartsGroup. In this example, the user will be viewing the data through five "relational hops."

Jumping through four or five or more relational hops to view or edit data puts a real strain on the FileMaker software, especially if you are accessing the database over the internet, using a remote FileMaker Server or FileMaker Cloud. Technically, this is a valid process, but it puts a real strain on FileMaker and can drastically slow performance.

My recommended process for this is to use a series of List View layouts to find the necessary records. These would be scripted to find the next set of related records on an additional List View layout.

> **OPINION**
>
> After reviewing this section of the manual, one of our longtime senior engineers who has been a developer for over 20 years, told me explicitly that he refuses to build part of an interface where you are displaying data with more than 3 table occurrence "hops" in it. In the example here, we talk about 5 hops, which clearly would be problematic.
>
> There have been performance tests by other senior members of the FileMaker community that show that this is overall a very detrimental design and causes a lot of unnecessary processing and overhead.

Working directly on the actual data and not through a relationship will provide the highest level of performance possible; and also minimizes the effort that the FileMaker Server has to make to display the information for you.

If you use a single layout design, then you will have to drill down through all of these relationships. When you want to add or edit a new part, the entire chain of related records will be locked from other users who want to edit the data.

For example, say I am adding parts for a 2014 Honda Pilot (Manufacturer is Honda, Year is 2014, Model is Pilot, PartsGroup is Engine and Part is muffler bearings). Now say another user wants to access and edit a part for a 2011 Honda Pilot, they will be unable to edit the record because the first user (me) has locked all of the records sequentially.

The Honda record, Year record, Model, PartsGroup and Part records are all locked. The second user cannot add or edit data on any Honda vehicle. So, while using a single layout with a lot of portals might seem like a cool technique, it has severe performance and multi-user issues.

File Naming

Imagine you have three clients and they all want contacts databases, so you name the file Contacts for all three clients. No problem, you have these files in the proper projects folders so they won't get confused, right? Wrong!

Bad things will happen when all three clients ask you to host their files on the web (and under other circumstances too).

Your web server and middleware software will be pointed at files with exactly the same name for three different clients, a recipe for disaster.

Always name your files in such a way that the file name also identifies the client:

- *ACME_Bomb_Disposal_fmsp.fmp12*
- *Mercury_Toyota_fmsp.fmp12*
- *Safeway_fmsp.fmp12*

In other words, the file name should always start with an abbreviated identifier for the company the file belongs to, or the project name, or both. No exceptions. This will also ensure that each client's files will sort together in your web server's folders, if clients have multiple files.

Don't Mix Techniques

For everything you want to accomplish in FileMaker there are a variety of techniques or approaches. For example: if you want users to be able to find specific records in a table, you can use a traditional find approach, or you can create a universal relationship from the table to itself, showing all the records in a portal where portal rows have a button over them that will navigate to that record.

Whether you choose one of these or some other technique, be certain you use the same techniques throughout the rest of your solution. Don't use one approach in part of your solution and a different approach in another. You will confuse your users.

Think Outside The Box

This has to do with the technical problems you will encounter as you develop your database, a subject this book is not really about, but which should perhaps be touched on here in a broad sense.

Most of the questions on the FMP related forums have to do with how do I? In other words, how do I implement this feature or function? Or, how do I structure my solution to handle this kind of data?

When faced with a problem, take the time to step back and view your solution from a distance as it were, and see it in broader terms. Abstract the things you are working with as much as possible. Peel back the layers of the problem at hand until you see the essence of the thing and the solution makes itself plain to you.

(Does this sound a little too existential?) For example:

> **FYI**
>
> One of the greatest demographics of FileMaker developers are developers who already have some sort of musical or creative talent.
>
> FileMaker gives you the opportunity to creatively problem-solve and this tends to appeal to those individuals who are generally more creative and who like to solve problems.
>
> As it turns out, the FileMaker community is heavily peppered with individuals who play piano or other instruments or have some sort of underlying creative talent, such as painting, writing, etc.
>
> FileMaker offers the ability to solve many different types of problems and it is up to your creative juices to work out a solution to the problem. Typically, there is more than one answer to a problem and as you gain more experience you will begin to see this.

In another section, I tell you not to allow creation of related records in portals then give you a way to script the creation of those records. But what if you can't go to a layout for the related table for some reason (as the script requires).

What then?

You have a relationship that will not allow the automatic creation of related records. You cannot create related records manually with a script, because you can't go to a related table occurrence layout. You need the automatic creation of related records, but can't have it with this relationship.

What do you do?

Well, if you have a relationship that won't let you do what you want, then create one that will let you do it.

Just duplicate the relationship, turn on *Allow creation of related records* in the duplicate relationship, and use that relationship for this single purpose. Just get the next serial number for the foreign key of your related table and plug it into the primary key field of your duplicate relationship. Then set any field in the related record to any value and voila, you're record is created and you never left the layout you were on.

Here's another example…

You need to show three completely different sets of data from three different tables in the same portal. Let's say that you want to click a button to show a contact's mailing addresses in the portal, click another button, the mailing addresses disappear and the portal now shows phone numbers. Yet another button causes the phone numbers to vanish and email addresses appear.

How can you do this?

We know that a portal can only show data from one table, because it is a one-relationship object (in modern versions of FMP, you can show fields from tables further down the line in the same TO group, but that won't help here).

Since we can only see data from one table in a portal, then we'll put all of our three classes of related data into that one table. You now have all three tables, addresses, phones, and email addresses contained in a single table. All that remains is a way to view them separately as you click portal selection buttons.

For your portal, create a normal ID# to ID# relationship from your primary table to the multi-purpose table. Then add another key pair to the relationship.

In your primary table the key field is a global number field.

In the multi-purpose table the foreign key field is a stored calc: 1 if the record is an address, 2 if a phone number and 3 for email.

Stack your address, phone and email fields on top of each other in the portal. Then to change what is seen just have scripts insert a 1, 2 or 3 into the global primary key field. Your portal will show records from three completely different *tables*.

Of course you shouldn't add or edit records in this triple purpose portal, but we've already discussed that. I'll leave you to determine for yourself how to add, edit and delete these related records.

Just think outside the box and you'll figure it out.

Programmer Control of Data Entry

Some years ago I took on a client who, to say the least, got taken to the cleaners by his previous developer. The client had paid a lot of money for a set of databases that were an amateurish mess. By the time he began to suspect he hadn't gotten what he paid for, the programmer was nowhere to be found.

I had the sad duty of informing him that the databases he had were simply unsalvageable. His pride was doubly injured when he realized that my charges to build the solution properly were going to be substantially less than what he had already paid for the unworkable solution.

Absolutely nothing in these files was properly built. They weren't even close. But the thing that stuck most in my mind was the amount of data contained in the tables that was unusable due to a complete lack of control over data entry.

Remember this while you are creating fields: whatever users can do wrong, they will do wrong. If you don't control data entry tightly, when it comes time to move that data to new tables, create reports, sort records or perform any of a variety of other tasks, you may find yourself in big trouble.

The data in the aforementioned tables was so badly jumbled that no amount of clever scripts and calcs could possibly prepare it for transfer to a better format. It all had to be moved by hand.

For example: most of us use calcs or custom functions to format phone numbers. You can't put a phone number in a number field because phone numbers have parentheses and dashes and spaces, etc. So you must put a phone number in a text field.

Most of you probably know about custom functions that neatly format phone numbers for you. But that is not enough. What is to prevent a user from entering two phone numbers in the same field? And what about extensions? If you have only a phone number field, users will tack on extensions in that field. You can easily remove the letters e, x and t in your custom function, but the extension is a number. That will stay and mess up your calc. Give users a field for extension numbers and throw up a red flag if those aforementioned letters are in the phone number field.

And what about dates in text fields? There may at times be a reason to put a date in a text field. At the moment I can't think of one, but it has been done. A date in a text field can be converted to a real date. However, if that field contains dates such as: May 2003, 1.1.04, 2-2-2002, 3/3/03, 4|4|2005, 2001; you face a genuine brain bender. If users are allowed to place dates in a text field, this is exactly the kind of mess you will get.

One way to avoid this kind of data disaster is to make certain users have a place to put any kind of out-of-the-ordinary data they may have. For example, the solution mentioned above had phone numbers in some of the name fields. Why? Because some of the people for whom data was tracked had extra phone numbers. Users had no place to put them so they tacked them onto the name field in different formats, no less. Other name fields had two names in them because there were two people in charge instead of one. And some name fields had two names and two phone numbers in them. How on earth do you transfer that into your new file? You can't foresee every possible need for variations in data input, but there is a simple answer.

Most solutions will have a provision for notes. Put a small button next to fields likely to require data variations. The button adds a note to a notes portal and an asterisk graphic over itself. From then on, clicking the button takes the user directly to the note. Put the variation in the note instead of in the field. Problem solved. It's just like reading a book: if you see an asterisk you look to the bottom of the page for additional information.

Users will also simply put data in the wrong field: a last name in a first name field, a city name in a zip code field or an email address in a phone number field. You can't code for every eventuality, but you can head off the most common data input snafus.

There is one benefit to be had from the kind of data mess this client had. You can easily see what mistakes in data entry the solution's users tend to make, and you can also see how they want to enter data as compared to what the present system permits. Use the mess to help determine how your solution will control and organize data entry. For example: if the first name field has a lot of last names in it, and users want to enter the last name first... make sure they can. If you consistently find city names in zip code fields, ask users why this happens. They will always have a logical explanation. Then remove that logic.

Tab Based Layout Navigaton

If you've been following the advice in this book, then you are faced with the dilemma of navigating your users between layouts and will realize that you need some sort of tab navigation system.

(I am not talking about FMP *tab object*, which is something entirely different.)

A tab navigation system must have specific characteristics to work, both technically and visually, and you must get the logic of this right or you will spend a great deal of time fixing work you've already done. (Or perhaps not being able to fix it at all.)

You can place your top-level-hierarchy set of tabs across the top of your layouts (most common), vertically along the left side (next most common), along the right side (OK, but less common still), or along the bottom of the layout (bad design, don't do this).

Wherever that top-level-hierarchy set of tabs is located, it must remain identical throughout all of your user-accessible layouts (except those intended to be opened in secondary windows).

> **FYI**
>
> RCC has a FileMaker UI Design Course where we address these topics specifically. Our world-renowned UI designer, Nick Hunter, has very specific ideas on how design should be.
>
> His design skills are based on his work while at Apple and at FileMaker Inc.
>
> Check out the video course here:
>
> http://www.learningfilemaker.com/ui.html

If you have a top level tab set that looks like:

Then when users click on the Chico tab, you want to see:

NOT,

OK, go ahead and laugh, but I've seen this. A lot! In fact, in the space of just a few weeks I once examined six databases for potential clients and ALL exhibited this behavior (hence the idea to add this topic to the FileMaker Manual). How do you end up with that last set of tabs?

Easy you don't take the time to design your database in advance, and you don't build your layout and navigation system first. You'll quickly slide right into a conundrum just like this one. Once you've created a tab and a label for it, that tab must occupy exactly the same position on every layout, and the label must never change. And most importantly, that tab must always take you to the same layout.

> **FYI**
>
> While good planning is the hallmark of a great database design, frequently additional sections of a database app will be added as customer's needs mature. Therefore, while avoiding UI inconsistencies is important, it may not be possible.

You can darken or highlight the tab to show it is selected, and you can alter the style or color of the label text as another form of indicator. But you must never move or change either.

What was missing in the aforementioned six databases was the understanding (born of proper design) that would have told the developer that Lucy and Co. were actually a second-level tab group:

Since it is significantly more difficult to create a navigation system with two levels of tabs (not to mention, three, four or five levels), novice developers naturally try to build everything on a single level. It can't be done. If you have one level of tabs, you must have two or more.

Go back up the page and take a look at the last example. Notice how both Chico and Lucy are in bold text, indicating they are both selected tabs? Can you see what's happening here?

Once you create a second-level tab set, the layout for the parent first-level tab becomes a second-level layout. The first-level tab no longer has a layout. In fact there is no Chico layout any longer. Neither is there a Lucy layout. There is only a Chico-Lucy layout. Clicking on either tab will take you to the same single layout.

There are separate layouts for the Ricky, Ethel and Fred tabs. But let's say we want a third level of tabs:

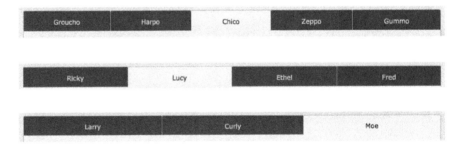

Now there is no Chico layout, no Lucy layout and no Moe layout. There is only one layout among these three tabs, the Chico-Lucy-Moe layout.

Now suppose you have built lower-level tab sets under all of the top-level tabs: Groucho, Harpo, Chico, Zeppo and Gummo. This would mean there are actually no top-level layouts corresponding to your five top-level tabs, because each has defaulted to a lower-level layout and each upper level tab is now just a bookmark for a series of layouts below it in the hierarchy.

Does your brain hurt yet? Walk away from it and come back tomorrow.

You'll get it. In the mean time, think about how impossible it would be to do this correctly without prior planning! Now you can see how easily Lucy's crowd got all jumbled up with Groucho's gang.

For practice, sit down with a legal pad (DO NOT do this on the computer) and make up a hierarchy of tabbed layouts for an imaginary database. You'll be surprised just how difficult this can be. Make it at least three levels deep and write down what data is going to be visible on each layout. You should have quite a respectable pile of crumpled yellow paper on the floor before you've finished.

When you're done, think about how nearly impossible it would have been to try to make a database work with only your first draft of this experimental hierarchy, because that's exactly what you're doing when you just dive right in and start coding without a strong design for your solution.

When it comes time to plan a layout and hierarchy scheme for a real project, do it exactly this way…

Always on paper first. Don't quit when it's good. Keep going until it's perfect. Only then should you fire up FileMaker.

Data, Logic and Layout Design

For years I took the same approach to building databases. First I would build the logic of the solution, then I would design and build the layouts. My rationale was that the logical structure dictated the design of the layouts and therefore had to be built first. I would make temporary dummy layouts as I worked, then fix them later.

Some years ago while working on several projects with one of my mentors, he insisted that I build the layout structure first, then the logic. I balked at this and needed some convincing. He pointed out that he was the project director, I was just the programmer, and projects were going to be done his way. His reasoning seemed flawless to me so I complied.

Put another way, the project director knew the business workflow and he wanted that workflow to dictate the layout design.

With a lot of trepidation I started building projects, layouts first. I was certain this approach made no sense whatsoever, but as I worked I got more and more comfortable with the idea. Today I start every project, layouts first. I can't really explain why this approach is more advantageous. You have to do it to understand it. But it does force you to think about the logic of your solution from a different perspective before you build it. All I can say is that it helps, and seems to prevent a lot of needless restructuring of the database logic later.

NOTE FROM RICHARD

The reason this worked for David was at this point in his career, he already had a great deal of experience. From this experience, David was able to mentally understand and design the structure of a database system.

You too will be able to design a system from the layout-side first; once you have sufficient experience. As you gain experience, your brain (whether you know it or not) will work out the backend structure, at a subconscious level.

After all these years of experience, my brain tends to do this automatically.

When you can do this, you truly are a FileMaker Jedi.

Building the layout and navigation system first is a better approach, at least for me. On the other hand, I was right too. The logic of your solution does dictate layout design and you may have to change some designs based on various nuances of the logic. It boils down to a chicken and egg sort of conundrum, either side of which can be correct at any given time (as Richard said, this is made much easier with additional experience).

At this point you must be thoroughly confused about what all this has to do with the title of this section. (Come to think of it, I'm getting a little confused myself!) Let me see if I can create a transition here that isn't too bumpy:

Logic dictates layout design. But layout design also influences logic. You may have to change the logic of your solution to accommodate the type of layout you want to use. There is one other previously unmentioned factor that will help us get where we're going… Data. Data dictates both database logic and layout design!

The fact that the type of data you need to handle will influence the logical structure of your solution is not exactly a revelation. Everyone figures that out early on. But the fact that data also dictates the design of your layouts isn't quite so obvious to many. Now comes the subtlety we're trying to reach.

When you realize that data dictates layout design and layout design influences logic, we've come full circle. Data controls the structure of your solution from two directions: it's direct influence over logical structure; and indirectly via its control over layout design, which layout design in turn influences logical structure. An example is really in order here:

I recall working on a particular preexisting solution that had to be redone from the ground up. The existing solution was completely unworkable because the logical structure of the database had little to do with the data that users were actually storing in it.

One of the biggest problems was notes. There were three generic note fields in each record. Presumably, the programmer added the extra fields when he realized additional notes were required and he didn't know he could build a related table for notes.

Most FMP programmers don't have to work with databases very long before they realize that notes should generally be kept in a separate table and viewed/added/deleted by means of access through a relationship/portal. This way extra fields don't have to be added to a solution each time a new note is required. This is pretty basic stuff. Put a notes field portal at the bottom of the layout somewhere and you're done. But it isn't always the correct approach.

FileMaker Jedi you will become, when you master this material.

In this particular case, a lot of notes were stored somewhere other than the three notes fields. In the contacts section of the database, two names were sometimes placed in the name field if two people shared the same responsibilities. If their company was unconventional in some way, the note information describing this difference was added onto the end of the more conventional data stored in the *CompanyType* field.

In this case, the data contained in the original file is trying to tell us something. There are three note fields on the layout, but users are putting some note data into fields that have nothing to do with notes. They are tacking this data onto the ends of specific, existing data fields obviously intended for other purposes. Why?

Users had three note fields to choose from, with a jumble of disconnected data in each. Finding the name of that second person in charge, or a description of the subtlety with regard to the type of company described in one of those three note fields would have been a constant nuisance. For all practical purposes the data would have been lost. Users realized this intuitively and put their note information into the most closely relevant data fields instead of the note fields available so they would have instant access to the non-conventional information about each field in question. (Of course if it was this simple, an extra name or company description field might have solved the problem, but there was actually a sea of disjointed information tacked onto these fields.)

To look at this data mess one would tend to think, *these users need a slap on the wrist; they are putting data everywhere but where it belongs.* But the reality is that they were intuitively putting the data exactly where it belonged, had the solution been constructed properly. Data was attempting to dictate logic and layout design! The programmer just wasn't paying attention.

If the solution had instead been designed with a portal for notes, it would not have been any better: just neater. Users would still have tacked certain notes onto the end of data fields instead of using the notes portal, because using the notes portal would mean having to search through it every time users wanted to see any of these data nuances. Worse, having this information in a portal would necessitate searching through the portal just to discover if there were any existing notes that qualified the data in the other fields. The data fields themselves would give no indication that a qualifying note existed or where in the portal it was to be found. So what was to be done?

Remember, data is dictating layout design. In this case the solution requires notes that are visibly associated with some of the data fields, not disconnected in a notes portal at the bottom of the layout. Data is also dictating logic: the type of information tacked onto the end of these data fields is singular in nature. Multiple notes for each field are not required. Finally, layout design is influencing logic: adding a note field next to each data field on the layout is out of the question. There is not enough room on the layout and if there were, the layout would look far too cluttered and confusing. Notes have to be both hidden and visible at the same time (so that users know at a glance when there are associated qualifying notes for a field).

To solve the problem, a separate note field was created for each relevant data field in the same table as the data. These note fields were the same width on the layout, but set to a greater length. The note fields were set to disallow entry and then hidden behind their relevant fields on the layout. A checkbox button was placed next to each visible data field and a calculation field placed over it to display a checkmark if the note field contained text. Clicking on the button went to the hidden note field in question, bringing it into view. Users had only to see a checkmark to know there was a note relevant to that field. A notes portal and table were also added for general information that was unrelated to specific fields.

So, what is to be learned here?

If users are making a mess of data and are not using, or are misusing certain features, don't assume it's because they're all as dumb as a box of hammers. Perhaps data is trying to dictate database logic and layout design and your users are trying to bend your solution to work the way the data wants it to.

IMPORTANT →

If you can't figure out how to organize a layout, don't just make the layout bigger or add another tab or portal. Look at the logical structure of your solution and the data it will handle to see if they indicate what to do.

If your logical structure just isn't coming together, flesh out your layouts as much as possible to see if they will help indicate to you how to alter your database logic.

Each of these three things; data, logical structure, and layout design are interdependant. If you're stuck, chances are that one of these things is trying to tell you something about the others. Pay attention to it!

Remember That It's All About the Data

It may seem like we are beating a dead horse about the overuse of graphics in a FileMaker application. However, this is one of the capabilities that new developers tend to discover, and they love to incorporate images into their FileMaker application. Keep in mind; the focus has to be on the data, not the pretty pictures contained within the FileMaker file. If you have a high-resolution image that becomes the backdrop of your application, then you must understand the background image has to download to each of your users every time they open up the file or change layouts.

When you start a new project with a blank FMP file, you already have one table and one layout. If you add one simple text or number field and then quit, at that point you have built the world's fastest FileMaker database. From there, it's all downhill!

Every field, calculation, script, layout, table, graphic, custom function or anything else you add after that first field, slows down your database. Of course a one-table, one-layout, one-field solution isn't good for much of anything and fortunately you can add quite a bit before there is any detectable slow down (otherwise FMP wouldn't be of much use). But the point is that everything you put in comes at a price.

If you put a graphic on the layout, it takes time for FMP to draw it. A calc field takes time to perform its calculation. You want to make sure you need everything you add because even a moderate solution requires quite a bit of "overhead" to perform all its vital tasks and should not be required to devote time to tasks that do not add to the usefulness of the solution.

If you are new to FileMaker, one of the first things you will/have discovered is that the simple database you decided to build turned out to be far more complex than you anticipated. In addition to a few simple tables, fields, relationships and layouts to manage your data, you needed scripts to navigate between layouts or create reports, controls over data entry, lots of calculation fields to manipulate basic data for special needs and a host of features to make the data more useful. In any database, the tables and basic data fields are the smallest part of the solution. It is the rest of the solution, the overhead, that grows exponentially. It is this overhead that makes a solution large and uses up clock cycles. You'll need a lot of it, and you don't want any that isn't essential.

Changing a background image using a PNG, JPG, or other official graphic adds overhead to a solution. If adding UI design elements improves the simplicity and understanding of the application, then make sure you do so by using lightweight and efficient graphics (like the SVG file format images). As a side note, if you use a ton of conditional formatting or the 'hide object feature' you

FYI

From a novice perspective, it should be assumed a image will be downloaded from the network everytime it is displayed. However, a senior engineer will understand that there are times when images are cached at the client level.

TERMINOLOGY

"Overhead" = network bandwidth. This also means, if you have a lot of it, it is going to suck.

TERMINOLOGY

"Object hiding" is actually known as POV or Programmatic Object Invisibility. POV happens to be a trademarked term so FileMaker Inc. (FMI) does not use it in any of their manuals or literature, but that is a more accurate name for that feature.

are going to add additional performance overhead to the FileMaker file. Make sure to use these processes sparingly, as needed, to help improve the user's understanding of the application. Pasting a large image into the background of your application is one feature that could slow your application to a crawl.

Always remember that you are building a tool. If a feature doesn't make the tool work better, leave it out, because each additional feature carries the potential to make the tool work less well. A hammer is no more useful as a hammer if you tie a bright ribbon around it.

This is not to say you should create plain, black and white layouts with no color or design to them. An attractive, well-designed layout does make the tool more useful, because it makes it easier for users to relate to the data the layouts present. However, once you move past attractive, practical and easy on the eye to multiple background color choices, dancing icons and movie-style fade-ins, you've gone too far.

Earlier in this book I mentioned that one of the first things to do when starting a project is to get your hands on your client's logo. This logo has a color scheme and must (usually) appear on every layout. The color scheme of your layouts has to blend with your client's logo. It is unlikely you can provide any variety of significantly different background color options that will also blend well with that logo. It's silly to try. Create one layout color scheme that looks good with your client's logo, get your client's approval and then forget about it. There is absolutely no need for additional color options or the overhead they require.

All useless features you add to a solution take time to implement. If someone is paying you for that time, they are not going to be thrilled with the cost of Technicolor background options, or any other unnecessary feature you've taken time to add. That client will not feel they've gotten good value for their money and you will look bad. You'll look far worse if the client realizes the solution is also too slow.

Custom Themes and Shared Styles

Introduced with FileMaker 12 was the idea that each layout has a theme and within that theme are the various styles or elements that make up all of the objects on the layout. The most important takeaway is that you can make your FileMaker application download across the network at least twice as fast by using "custom themes" and "shared styles."

It is probably better that you watch our videos on this topic because it can be a little bit taxing to try and explain this in writing. The short version is that when building an application, pick a single theme to leverage, then define styles for the items on the layout.

For example, on a Contacts data entry screen, the name, address, city, state, zip, shipping and all of those standard fields, should have the same styling. If you click on each field and individually style it, you are loading extra invisible CSS code into your FileMaker file, slowing it down. The best idea is to first style one common element correctly and save the style. Then apply that style to all of the similar elements.

So you would set up the First Name field, style it the way you want and save that style. Then apply that style to all of the data entry fields on that layout. You would do the same thing for buttons.

The main takeaway is; if you click on each field and style it, you are not sharing the code. You are creating new invisible CSS code for each one. Doing this can double the 'under the hood' code that FileMaker uses to render the layout.

We have done real tests with this a few years back using data analysis tools to measure the amount of traffic going over the network, for a layout to be rendered. By using a custom theme and shared styles for the common elements, we lightened the load of the of the layout download by half. So, you could then assume that the download was twice as fast.

VIDEO TIP - 17 PLATFORM VIDEO COURSE
To learn more about Custom Themes and Shared Styles, watch video "0601 - Making Layouts load 200% faster - Performance".

Leave a Trail of Bread Crumbs

Document everything.

Without complete documentation, whether you are a novice developer or seasoned pro, I can absolutely guarantee that when you go back a month or two later to make changes to your solution, you will not be able to understand what you did or why.

Even the simplest solutions can seem impenetrable just a few weeks after the fact.

Leave a trail of bread crumbs (thorough comments for every field, script, etc.) in your solution, or face having to reverse engineer your own work: embarrassing at best. In addition, have complete written documentation of your project. This may all seem like a lot of extra work, but it actually means much less work in the long run.

If you use a field or script naming convention, and you should, be sure to document it also. If you don't write it down, you may forget why a group of field names starts with q or ends with z.

Every project, when complete, should be accompanied by an extensive document detailing every aspect of your database design. You will need it, and it will save you many hours of head scratching. It's also a professional touch that impresses clients.

Organize your fields, scripts and value lists into labeled groups. Create unused global fields, empty scripts or empty value lists, and name them in such a way that they indicate what is underneath them. You can break the naming rules with these items because they are only labels and will not be used anywhere. So spaces, punctuation, etc., are all OK.

For example: if you group all your primary key fields together, create a global number field titled --Primary Keys--. Put it at the top of the group of primary key fields. Create an empty script called --Navigation Scripts--. Group all your navigation scripts together and place the empty script at the top of the list. Make your lists of fields, scripts and value lists neat, orderly and self-explanatory. You get the idea. You'll thank yourself later.

Make Certain You Have at Least One Record

This is another one of those things that can cause you embarrassment when you deploy a solution.

There are lots of reasons, too many to go into here, that you would want a solution to contain at least one record when you deliver it. Some things just won't work or function correctly if there are no records present.

If yours is the kind of solution you will deliver empty of records, test it that way before you deliver it. Make sure everything works without any records present.

If it doesn't work, add a routine to your startup script that checks for the number of records. If that number is zero, the startup script creates a record and performs whatever tasks may be necessary to prime your solution and make certain the blank record it created doesn't stay around forever.

Another approach some have taken is to leave a sample record(s) in the database when delivered. Routines are added to the delete record scripts that will not allow the last remaining record to be deleted, so the user must add his own record before the sample can be deleted.

Of course, this is also another reason not to allow users access to menus. If your solution will not work properly with no records present and users have the ability to show all records and delete all records, you could have a problem.

SAMPLE FILE

This should be part of your "Pre-Launch Checklist". Check out a sample pdf here:

http://bit.ly/FMSPLaunchChecklist17

In addition, even with records in the database, make certain everything works with a found count of zero, if it is possible for your user to end up with that found count.

There are also occasions when a layout must always show at least one found record. Your scripts must prevent having a found count of zero.

Test Your Solution Often

Imagine you have invested 200 hours in a project that is now near completion and it is time to deploy it for testing. You happily announce to your boss that the project is almost done and is ready for deployment. You set up the server, install the user stations, import your company data into your tables, take the system online and voila! Your database is not moving quite as quickly as the glacier outside your window.

You forgot to frequently test your solution while developing it, with real data in the quantities it would be expected to handle.

Whatever the reason, whether you loaded the solution down with too many unstored calcs, too many plugins, too many cute and clever tricks, too many complicated keys, or too many graphics, you didn't spot it and now you look bad, very bad, and very publicly. Recovery of your credibility is unlikely.

In order to avoid having to update your resume unexpectedly, test your solution thoroughly at every step along the way. And if it looks like it is getting sluggish, start throwing unnecessary items overboard and otherwise looking for ways to speed everything up.

Remember, FileMaker is both an interface and a database. There is an inverse relationship between how much data FileMaker can handle swiftly and how complicated your interface may be. The more data FileMaker has to handle (and it can handle quite a lot) the more it will be slowed by being top-heavy with too much extra baggage.

I recommend you spend some time developing your solution while it is running on a FileMaker Server. Once deployed with real users, it will provide excellent feedback regarding what the real-world performance reflects.

I also recommend importing a large volume of real data, as well as accessing the FileMaker server across the internet. This gives you a feel for the actual performance and will help avoid a lot of pitfalls.

FYI

To best simulate user experience, make sure your database is running on a FileMaker Server at a remote location (or use FileMaker Cloud). Also, make sure to load a large block of sample data to simulate real-world performance.

TERMINOLOGY

"Stakeholders" are the people who have a financial interest in a good outcome of a development project. Sometimes they are the end-users; sometimes they are not.

IMPORTANT →

Watch for Gotchas

This is a forest for the trees topic that is very important. It is super important that your end users and "stakeholders" frequently review ongoing development and provide feedback.

In an ideal world, you would complete Section 1 of a new custom application for them to review. You would then move on to build Section 2. While you are building Section 2, the end users (or stakeholders) can provide you with feedback on Section 1. You can go back and address the issues that they have identified as problematic. At a very simplistic level, this methodology is called "Agile Development."

The important part of this process is that the end user or stakeholder spends the time to review the software during the development cycle. If the customer is busy doing their "day job," they will not take the time to frequently review the software and provide the feedback that you desperately need.

So, a critical part of a project's success is getting timely, continuous engagement by the customer to review your work and provide feedback. Here are some examples of feedback that we have seen with customers in the past:

- *If you have a portal listing all the attendees to a meeting, and a popup list for selecting people to add to that meeting, each time you select someone new to attend the meeting, their name should disappear from the popup list. After all, they are already scheduled for the meeting, so if their name still appears in the popup selection list, users will be confused.*
- *You might have a list of contact names in a portal on one side of your layout that you use to select their records for viewing and editing. Clicking on a portal row runs a script that places that contact's information into editing fields on the layout. Users will become confused if at the same time the information is loaded into the fields, the portal row they just clicked is not highlighted.*
- *A variation of the above: Your portal is alphabetically filterable so that you can limit it to display only contacts whose last names begin with a specific letter. If a user is viewing all the contacts whose name begins with B, and then decides to create a new contact record for someone whose name is Smith, that name will not appear in the portal. This can be confusing for a user who expects to see a new entry appear.*
- *As mentioned under Record Editing in Portals, portals that can be entered or edited can look very unprofessional, but so can portals that cannot be entered. One reason for this is that data can cause the text in a portal to appear misaligned when the text is too long for the field. For example, if your portal displays a list of names and one name is longer than the space provided in the field, the text that is visible will appear*

more toward the top of the field than data in other fields. This looks very sloppy. Create a stored calc strictly for displaying the name in the portal that gets only the left x number of characters of the name field so that data displayed in the portal will never be too long.

- *Clicking a button runs a lengthy script that does not warn, or give any indication to the user that the process may take some time.*
- *If you must have a portal that allows creation of related records, it is poor design and misleading to the user to see a trashcan or other icon on the last portal row where there is no data. (Hint: use a calculation field to show or hide the icon.)*

These are the kinds of things that seasoned developers will spot right away, but you as a novice developer won't have that advantage. To help find these things, you need to have your end user willing to look at your software as it develops and point the gotchas out to you. Even better, watch them work with the software so you can see for yourself when and where they get confused or misled.

Table Occurrences

Wrapping your brain around the concept of table occurrences (TO's) seems to be more difficult for those of us who started out with version 6, or earlier, of FileMaker than it is for those who came after. However, it is not easy for anyone. The simplest advice I can give is this:

Tables are the actual real-world containers of your data, *but* you can never access them directly. Think of your data as being safely stored away in locked vaults that just happen to be called *tables*. You may not touch them. Like a venomous snake in the zoo however, you may look at them from safety through a glass window. In this case, the glass window is a called a *table occurrence* and you can have as many windows into your data as you like.

The table occurrence also provides an advantage, not just a barrier. Unlike the glass at the zoo which is flat, clear and ordinary, a TO can be any kind of *glass* and allow you to look at your data in as many different ways as you have table occurrences. You can look at your data through frosted glass, colored glass, rippled glass, etc. (OK, I'll drop the silly glass analogy.)

You can also think of TO's as being similar to *aliases* (shortcuts on Windows) that allow you indirect access to your tables. Each TO can have a different point of view, and a different view into other TO's in the same group of table occurrences. Since you can have more than one group of TO's you can have multiple groups with completely different perspectives on your data.

> **FYI**
> SQL developers may recognize a Table Occurrence as somewhat similar to a "view".

VIDEO TIP - 17 PLATFORM VIDEO COURSE

If you are confused then go watch the pencil/bridge video "0315 - What is a Relationship? (Very Basic Video)".

Also found on Youtube:

https://youtu.be/WXJuSNyVcTs

The tendency of some when they first start to explore FileMaker is to presume that the first TO for a table, the one FileMaker creates for you automatically for each new table, is somehow the *real* table, and the others are somehow copies. This is not the case. That first TO is just exactly the same as all the others you will create. FileMaker just creates the first one for you as a courtesy. There is no *real table* occurrence in the Define Database relationship dialog. You could if you wished, delete all table occurrences and your tables would still be there, intact. You simply would not be able to access your data, and that is the central point: TO's are for viewing and manipulating data. They are your means of reaching into and altering or displaying your data. They are not the actual data tables.

User Settings

User settings that must be retained from session to session cannot be stored in global fields as mentioned previously. If you know your database(s) will have multiple users, or if you have the slightest suspicion that it might one day have more than one user, always build a Preferences table into your solution.

Keep in mind; there are two types of settings you are likely to save: System-wide and Individual User settings.

System-wide settings would be stored in a Preference table. A Preference table only has one record in it.

For Individual User settings, the ideal location for saved preferences is a Staff or User table, to which you will want to add additional fields.

In an ideal world, these records would also correspond to the different security accounts contained within the FileMaker Security dialog. There is no automatic connection between a Staff/User table and the FileMaker Security dialog. Either you or the developer must manually handle the dialog via a script.

A classic example of a user setting is one where we track the preferred location and size of a calendar the user likes to display. During the startup script that always runs, we know the ID of the user who is logged in. With that information, we can quickly find that user in the Staff/User table and grab the relevant preference data from that record, then load those preference settings into global variables.

Then we use the global variables to manage the behavior of the FileMaker application for the user during the session. When the user decides to close or exit the FileMaker application, we run a final Close script. This Close script writes any user-specific preference settings back to that user's individual Staff/User record.

Always think of the users of your database as being simply another kind of data you must track, therefore requiring their own table. There is no other place to put this kind of information. Each user will have a permanent record in the Staff/User table and their particular settings are stored there in standard, not global fields. This way the data is always available and you needn't worry about volatility.

Only if your database won't have any users at all (including you), can you exclude a preferences table.

In summary, you will have a single record in a Preference table, and multiple records in a Staff/User table.

> **IMPORTANT**
> If you are using a "User" table then the Startup script should identify the correct user based on their account name and then load critical user settings into global settings for later use within scripts.

Reports Tables

All FileMaker novices think of reports in a one-dimensional manner. That is, they think of them as ephemeral; temporary organizations of data meant to be printed (or viewed) and then discarded with the only record of their having existed residing on a printed page or solely in the mind. Often, a more permanent snapshot of the database is needed. For this you will need one or more reports tables.

Two driving issues dictate the creation of dedicated report tables. The first issue, of course, is the idea of preserving data to be referenced in the future.

The second issue is when you construct a report that takes a long time to generate and become visible. The technical term is "processor intensive." In this case, you want to have the reports pre-created and saved into a dedicated table.

Pre-created reports will leverage number and text fields, not calculation fields. The idea is, you run a script that does all the calculations in advance (before the user asks for it). Those calculations save in text and number fields, so they do not have to be re-calculated in the future.

Now as you can tell, most all the topics in this book relate to each other. If you remember the conversation from a few pages ago, we were discussing user feedback. Well, if you are getting continuous user feedback and you build a report that takes forever to generate, your users will start squawking and complaining. Once this happens, you know that you need to process the reports offline and have the results saved in number and text fields.

> **TERMINOLOGY**
> "Processor Intensive" is the technical term for a task that slows a computer. This generally makes the users grumpy while waiting for their computers.

VIDEO TIP - 17 PLATFORM VIDEO COURSE

To learn more about a dedicated Robot computer, watch video "1915 - What is a FileMaker Robot?".

The process of generating the report offline is handled best with a dedicated robot computer. Some people like to use the FileMakers server to run the report scripts. However, you can get into trouble with this kind of process, leaving parts of the server non-functional. We will cover that in the Robots section of this book.

If the report is pre-calculated (i.e., it is pre-cached and pre-saved) then all you have to do is find the necessary report records and display them as needed.

The other issue I mentioned at the top of this section is the idea that you want a permanent snapshot of the report for future references. To expand upon this idea, you are going to run into data systems where daily totals and calculations have to be run and preserved on a daily basis. Otherwise, the information will be lost. We have seen situations where activities of low importance occur during the day. There is not a great deal of logging that goes on to track them.

For example, RCC has a database to manage the people who are subscribed to our weekly video campaign. On a daily basis, a small number of these people unsubscribe because they do not wish to receive the emails. Historically, RCC does not track the totals of unsubscribes. This information is not critcal to the success of the company. However, if we decide that we do want to chart the rates of unsubscribers, we would build what we call a Daily Analytics table. The Daily Analytics table is where each record represents one calendar day. Conceptually, over many years, this table would grow to thousands of records. However, for one specific day, November 21, 2018, there would be a single record that would contain the totals of our unsubscribers, new people that subscribed, and totals of financial sales for that day, etc. All sorts of daily analytics can be calculated and saved on a daily basis and preserved for future reference.

To summarize, you are going to have situations where you want to preserve calculated report data. The database itself shows cumulative totals, not how that total has grown on a daily basis. You may want to preserve daily analytics for that. You want reports that are processor intensive, to be pre-calculated and pre-cached so a user can press a button and instantly display a report.

Random Number Generator

Elsewhere in this book I briefly discuss the random number generator in FMP. One day you are going to have a project for which you need to generate numbers as close to truly random as possible.

Imagine you've been hired by a State that has been newly admitted to the union (the State of Confusion for example) to build their lotto software (now required for admittance to the Union I believe). Then imagine it is discovered that your software does not select lotto numbers randomly at all, but rather exhibits a detectable pattern. Worse, the lottery was running for months before this was discovered. Brother… are you getting sued! FileMaker cannot generate enough zeros for what you're gonna have to pay!

Before you crunch down on that cyanide capsule (every software developer should keep one handy), there is a solution.

I won't get into the technical difficulties of random number generating routines and the subject of seed numbers, etc., mostly because you'd probably notice I don't really know what I'm talking about and that could prove embarrassing. So let's just move on to solving the problem (without having to know what we're talking about).

The random number generator in FileMaker doesn't work. The numbers it generates are not truly random and will be produced in an observable pattern. (It is important to stress that random does not mean unique! It is OK for a random number generator to produce the same number multiple times. It is not OK for it to produce numbers in a pattern, which by definition is not random.) Before you write a nasty letter to FMI, you should know that the same is true of every random number generator in every software package. None of them produce numbers that are truly random.

Depending on the circumstances, the generation of random numbers seems to be a bigger problem at some times that at others. The worst case I've ever seen occurred with a project of mine where I had to randomly checkmark some of the rows in a portal containing anywhere from 35-50 records. After running the random selection script about ten times, I noticed the routine consistently refused to select two groups of records in the portal: a group of about 8-10 records at the end of the portal list and another group of about 4-5 records located three rows from the top of the portal list. No matter how many times I ran the script these records were never selected. That is definitely not random!

I checked all the FMP mailing lists and forums for suggested random formulas to improve on my results. I found a few ideas, but the end result was that nothing worked. I either had to give up on the idea all together, or invent my own solution. Here it is:

Imagine you have a cat that insists on using your living room rug instead of the litter box. You can get him to use the box from time to time, but he really loves that carpet. The same is true of the FMP random number generator. It just seems to like certain numbers more than others. Well if you can't get the cat to stop going to the living room…

Move the living room!

And if you can't get FileMaker's random number generator to stop taking you to the same record…

Move the record!

Let's exaggerate the situation for a moment. Imagine that FMP always selects a random number that takes you to exactly the same record. Now there is no randomness at all. But if it always wants to go to record number three, just make sure record number three is a different record each time FMP acts.

Instead of trying to select random records in a portal I decided to go to the related records in their own table. There, in a field created just for this purpose, I looped through the records, setting that field in each record to a random number. Then I sorted the records by that randomly numbered field, followed by the random selection of a single record to be marked. Each time another record was to be marked, I put new random numbers into the aforementioned field (remember, they are still sorted by the last set of random numbers, so any pattern of numbers the random number generator might come up with would be foiled) and sorted the records again, then selecting another random record. This worked beautifully. There was no discernible pattern to record selection. The key to this is that each time a new record is selected, it is from a group of records that has been sorted by a random number, then sorted again by a random number before the next selection. This way, they are never sorted in the same order when they are again randomized.

Though I hesitate to say you can achieve true randomness this way, I certainly think you can get far better results than you are likely to need (I'll still give the lotto project a pass; it's yours if you want it).

The trick here is the idea of making a random selection from a constantly reordered random selection. No matter how persistently FMP's random number generator wants to take you back to the living room, it keeps getting to the location where it last found the living room only to find the bathroom, the kitchen, laundry room, anything but the living room!

If you feel you need even further randomization you only have to add another layer to this concept. For example: select a subset of records at random (one at a time), set their random number fields to a new random number, then sort again. Sort from ascending to descending for one selection then reverse it for the next.

There is no limit to how deeply you can nest this. Just keep that living room on the move and FMP's cat won't be able to soil the carpet.

Relevant to many of the other topics in this book there is a web site you ought to see. In particular, most of a very enlightening book is posted there: http://www.joelonsoftware.com/uibook/chapters/fog0000000057.html

Joel Spolsky is the author and a well-known software development writer. He also has a sense of humor, which doesn't hurt. Give it a read.

FYI

Historically, random number generators were based upon some advanced mathematics in the form of the Fourier Transform. As David notated in this section, over the years this has caused problems because the old school use of this function does not necessarily give you real random numbers. But it is pretty convincing, for most people, that it appears to generate random numbers.

The generation of real random numbers is critical to modern encryption; so this is more of a hot topic. Additional reading will indicate that there are many standards for UUID random generation.

For the technically-minded, FMI is using the RFC 4122 standard, version 4.

Read an article about this topic here:

http://bit.ly/UUID_Random17

Detailed Conversation:

http://bit.ly/UUIDDetail17

Closing Words on Database Design

The conversation in the previous section is mostly about the planning of a FileMaker application before construction. In an ideal world, this planning would be completed in advance. However, I can not think of any FileMaker custom application that was designed 100% upfront.

As the FileMaker solution develops, project requirements tend to evolve especially if there is frequent user feedback. Therefore, a supercritical recommendation from me would be for you to think about periodic documentation and cleanup of your FileMaker solution.

For example, we have a free FileMaker application called FM Starting Point. Every 3-6 months new features are proposed for this product and existing features are potentially redesigned, rebuilt or maybe even removed. As a result, script numbering will go out of sequence, layout numbering and organization may become less organized, and scripts may not be commented on as fully as I would like.

Part of our post-development cleanup process is to do a "code review" with several FileMaker developers to ensure it meets our needs, and that proper documentation is added to the FileMaker scripts. A vast majority of the time when I do a code review I will hear something like, "I haven't commented on it yet; because I'm not sure it's the final fixed version of what I'm trying to build."

The reality is that some commenting needs to be done along the way by the developer. I understand that there will be some post-development cleanup. It is crucialy impotant that you ensure there is a dedicated cleanup process on the backend. During this cleanup and documentation process, everything is reviewed, and missing documentation is addressed. Remember to resequence your scripts and layouts with proper numbering and grouping.

Developers love to come sliding in on deadlines like a bunch of racers in the movie "The Fast and the Furious." Of course, a developer who is busy and just trying to make the minimum deadline is not going to be overly concerned about the documentation within the scripting.

If you are a developer, you need to be aware of this inherent human weakness and work to overcome it. If you are a manager, you should seriously enforce some draconian rules about the developers and documentation. Failure to do so will only lead to crying, heartache, and a lot of finger pointing down the road.

4 Database Design Errors

Separate Printing Layouts

Never print the layout in which your user enters data. Every FileMaker newcomer tries to print from his data entry layouts. It never works.

If a layout looks good for data entry or manipulation, it will look bad when printed. For anything you need to print, create a separate layout specifically designed for printing. Unless you allow the user to preview his document before printing, he should never even see the printing layout (you may occasionally wish to have yet a third layout just for previewing). Use a script to print; always. Freeze the window, go to the printing layout, execute the print command, return to the original layout.

Never, ever allow users access to the print command in FMP's standard File menu.

Never Print a Portal

Never, ever print a portal! Portals were not intended for printing, just viewing.

Of course, there are exceptions. In FM Starting Point, there are times when we print a portal. However, there is an underlying truth to many developers being reluctant to print portals.

Let us look at a typical Invoice and Invoice Line Items scenario. If you have a limited number of items on an invoice, then printing a portal is just fine. People do this all the time.

There are two rules to determine if you "should" print a portal:

    1) The text of the Line Items must be consistent in size.

    2) The Portal always stays on one page. It does not break across pages.

Another reason I like to print portals is that it is more useful in a training exercise when I am attempting to teach other FileMaker concepts. As a trainer, I want to keep any complexity limited to just the lesson I am trying to teach. For example, if I am teaching people about Line Items, then keeping the portal conversation simple is useful.

However, as you build real customer solutions, you need to remember the two rules listed previously. Your customers will end up needing an Invoice with more Line Items, than can fit on one page. Portals suck when printing across page boundaries. The customer will expect that their Invoice will print beautifully from one page to the next. Portals do not do this.

Typically a developer will manage the printing process by using a script. Of course, the easiest script to write is one that goes to a dedicated Invoice layout and just prints. Once again, for training, you will often see me print a layout with the portal on it.

You cannot use a portal if you have varying amounts of text from one portal row to the next or the portal breaks across a page.

For example, take a typical Invoice Layout which has Invoice Line items.

You will need to write a "print" script that goes to a printer-specific ListView layout. Once the script navigates to that location, it can execute a print command or save to PDF.

This printer-specific layout is based on the Invoice Line Items table occurrence (TO), which is different from the main Invoice with the portal on it. That layout is based on the Invoice parent record, and the portal shows the related Line Items.

So, to cleanly print more than one page of Line Items (i.e., a multi-page portal), we have to go to a ListView layout where the body part is not the Invoice parent but is the Invoice Line Item child.

In a situation like this, the information that is in the Header and the Footer (such as the Contact Name, etc.) is displayed relationally in fields on the Headers and Footers of the Invoice Line Items - List View layout.

A body part can expand or grow depending on the amount of data that is in that portal description. If you have portal Line Items with varying sizes of descriptions (from five words to hundreds of words), then printing the data using a body part will provide infinite flexibility (i.e., the body part can expand or grow).

Notice how the body part expands per Line Item in the screenshot on the next page.

In a portal, every line is sized identically and cannot grow based upon the contents of the records.

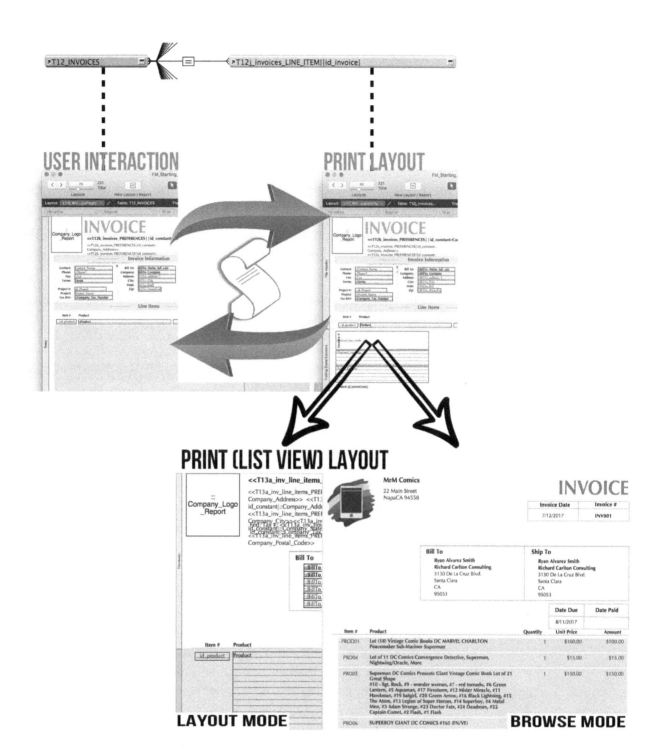

Cute & Clever Tricks

One of the first things FileMaker novices discover is the huge community of FMP developers willing to answer questions, provide advice, demos, sample solutions and support of any and every stripe. This is a wonderful support system and is very helpful to everyone, on many different levels.

Many advanced developers spend a lot of hours every year building demos and how-to instructions provided mostly free-of-charge or for a very nominal fee, to anyone who wants them. Some even provide free downloadable modules you can plug right into your solution. You'll never find a better community of colleagues anywhere. Of course they/we are all hoping you may hire them/us to help you over the rough spots but still, the generosity and openness cannot be denied.

However, some of these free techniques are not necessarily good options. There are many cute and clever things that can be done in FileMaker that are workable, but not practical. They may tend to slow your solution considerably, or limit options later.

Another limitation of some samples you may see is that the underlying sample file has a high degree of complexity which can be challenging to maintain.

For example, making a moving progress bar to show when a script is running. I have seen this done with container fields as well as web viewers. However, I will never use a web viewer unless I have to.

![Verify Batch of Emails against verify-email.org 50%]

Understand that FMI does not control the code that drives the web viewer. FileMaker references the operating system (Windows, Mac, Android, etc.) to display the contents of the web viewer. Each of these companies will write their HTML-rendering code differently. What makes this worse is, this code may have substantial, frequent changes.

For example, between the release of Pro 15 and Pro 16 on the Macintosh, the code that drove the web viewer was changed entirely by Apple.

If you had two sample demos that create a progress bar, I would never use the one with a web viewer (because of the volatility of that technology). In plain English, this means in the next release of FileMaker, your progress bar may not work, or it may look like dog doo-doo. However, FileMaker does control the code that drives container fields. Building a progress bar in a container will result in a much more stable and problem-free solution for years to come.

So, it is important to think about the people who will be supporting the solution and if they have the technical chops to support highly complex code.

Another example:

Matt Petrowsky has a significant number of very excellent demos in his ISO Magazine that are useful in learning about FileMaker. However, in one specific case, Matt has a demo of an unlimited number of related digital documents with the clever use of slide controls. This demo from

FILEMAKER JEDI REQUIRED

As a general rule, I highly recommend Matt Petrowsky. You can find him and his demo files at

http://www.filemakermagazine.com

Matt does not have the fragile weaknesses mentioned in the previous example, but it does take a FileMaker Jedi to understand that solution.

Chasing the Mouse

The way you choose to have users input data depends on the type, and particularly the amount, of data they will be entering.

If the nature of the solution you are building calls for users to be able to enter a lot of data quickly, having to go to the mouse is going to be very irritating and will slow users down drastically (giving them time to look for a rope and you).

During data entry, a user's hands should seldom, if ever, have to leave the keyboard.

Once again this gets back to the conversation we had previously about getting early, frequent feedback from end users about your solution. While we have not explicitly talked about user experience yet; it is the number one thing you are trying to enhance when building a FileMaker application. You want the user experience to be seemless and obvious, without requiring a lot of concentration and focus.

> **TERMINOLOGY**
>
> "User interface" (UI) is the graphical display of your FileMaker custom application. As a general rule, the user interface should be straight forward, self-evident and beautiful.
>
> People confuse "user experience" (UX) and "user interface." While UI is the level of beauty in the interface, the more important element to measure is whether the user has a positive or negative experience while using your solution (UX).
>
> A beautiful interface is worthless if its use is not self-evident. If the user has to read a manual to understand what is going on, you probably have a bad user experience.
>
> Good UI does not always equal Good UX.

Don't Use Single-Step Buttons

In the Specify Button dialog that appears after you create a new button, you have many options including the Perform Script step. Choosing any of the options in this dialog other than Perform Script creates a single-step button. Don't do it, ever!

If you need a button, create a new script for it and set the button to Perform Script. Even if that script will contain only one step, follow this rule always.

The primary reason for this is that virtually all single-step buttons end up requiring more steps, forcing you to create a script for the button anyway. This is simple labor saving advice born of experience. You cannot damage anything by creating single step buttons. You can (and will) only make a lot of extra work for yourself.

There are other reasons for not using single-step buttons. If for example, you have 20 layouts and a single-step button on each one that goes to layout X, the minute you need to change that to layout Y, you immediately have to change every button on all 20 layouts. If the buttons were instead all attached to a script that takes you to layout X, you need only change that one script.

Following this advice will save you a lot of time and aggravation. There is one exception however to the don't use single-step buttons rule. The Resume Script step is often and logically assigned to a single-step button in cases where users have to be taken to another layout/file temporarily and prevented from doing anything else by pausing a script until the required task is performed, and the single-step, Resume Script button is subsequently clicked.

Orphans are Okay

This is generally covered in most good FileMaker books but it is generally covered completely wrong.

In the relationship creation dialog, there are several options, including the Delete related records in this table when a record is deleted in the other table option. Be sure to review your relationships carefully. This option is left unchecked by default.

If you have a contact, for example, with related records in a phone number table, you would of course want those phone numbers deleted when you delete the contact. Otherwise you would have phone numbers that are not related to any contact, and in fact are inaccessible and simply occupying space in the table unnecessarily. These are commonly referred to as orphaned records.

If on the other hand, you have an invoice table, you would want Delete related records in this table when a record is deleted in the other table checked for the relationship to the line items table, but not for the relationship to the products table. When you delete an invoice (which according to strict accounting rules, you should never do), you want the line items to disappear with it. They are meaningless without the invoice to which they belong.

But, you do not want your entire product inventory to disappear every time you delete an invoice, so the Delete related records in this table when a record is deleted in the other table checkbox should be left empty for this relationship.

Based on this logic, you would want to turn on Delete related records. In some situations, that is a horrible idea.

There are two fundamental issues here that affect the process of "cascading deletes." The first issue is that FileMaker behaves in a very unexpected way with the cascading deletes enabled. If you look at the example screenshot below, you will see that we have two table occurrence groups (TOGs). Take a moment to review and understand this diagram. On the top TOG, we have the cascading delete turned on. On the bottom one, we have it turned off.

> **TERMINOLOGY**
> A "Table Occurrence Group" is defined as a group of Table Occurrences that are connected together, aka TOG.

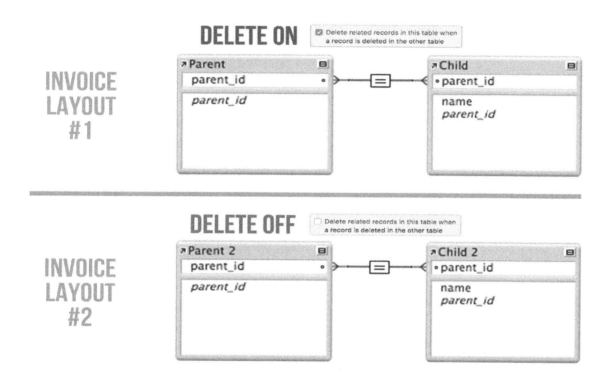

I know this sounds crazy, but if you are on Invoice Layout #2 (which is attached to the bottom TOG), and you delete the "Parent" record, it will not accept the cascading delete settings from that relationship.

The Parent 2 relationship says NOT to delete the record, this makes sense, except that FileMaker does not work that way.

FileMaker hunts through the relationships and sees that the cascading delete is enabled on the top TOG. So instead, it deletes the record. When I was updating this book, I was blown away to discover this, and verified this behavior with three different senior developers.

In plain English, this means that if the cascading delete is ON ANYWHERE between these two base tables, then the Child records are always going to be deleted.

> **TERMINOLOGY**
> "Cascading Deletes" is the industry common term (outside of the FileMaker world) for automatically deleting related records.

> **VIDEO TIP - 17 PLATFORM VIDEO COURSE**
> To learn more about the context of your scripts, watch video "0901 - Scripting".

This is extraordinarily dangerous for a wide variety of reasons. The biggest problem I have with this is that we always teach novice developers context is everything. When you are writing a script, the context of where you are at, what the Found Set is, and what the Sort Conditions are, are all highly relevant to the script's execution. Context is everything. This relationship is the one time where context is not everything; In fact, it is entirely ignored.

Of course, FMI would tell you that this is a feature (not a bug).

Now, take this odd behavior in conjunction with the fact that you are going to run into customers who swear their data is deleted out of their database.

"We put that data in last week, and now it is gone." When this happens, you are probably going to tell them that FileMaker does not delete data out of their database. They are going to swear that you are full of doo-doo. In a desperate attempt to find out what is deleting their data, you are likely to examine every Delete command in the database. Whether the Delete is in a script or in a relationship, you will turn it off. Then, the problem will magically go away.

This is an unnecessary customer hassle. If data needs to be deleted, you have to write a new record to the LOG Table, when you delete the record. That way you have some evidence that the record was deliberately deleted.

Because of this unusual behavior of performing cascading deletes, where cascading deletes are turned "OFF," my recommendation is NEVER to use them. It will help eliminate one source of complaints by a customer.

The downside to this process is, you may end up with records that are not relationally connected to anything else (i.e., "orphaned" records). These will take a minor amount of room in your solution. Allowing them to exist will never be a problem for anyone.

The exception to this, of course, would be for someone who is OCD. If you are obsessive-compulsive, you are likely to freak out with "orphaned" records living in your database.

Bottomline: not making orphans would be ideal, but not deleting critical data is WAY MORE important.

Mile-Long Popups

Novices are enamored of popup lists and menus. And justifiably so, because they are a handy tool and look very professional. However, you can get into trouble using them.

Before you decide to use a popup menu to solve a problem, ask yourself what the maximum number of entries that popup might contain. If it is more than 10-15 items (maximum), look for another approach, or find a way to filter the popup list. If you use a popup to select a record for example, and you have 200 records in that database, you will have a very long popup list indeed and users will hate it.

If you are married to using a long Value List, you should consider using the "Auto-Complete" feature. The Auto-Complete feature will help narrow a long List automatically.

Plugins

Avoid plugins like the plague. There will be rare occurrences when you absolutely, positively have to use one. Otherwise don't. If you can do the same thing with hours of tedious programming, do the programming. Don't use the plugin. If a plugin provides a feature you'd like, but can do without, Do without it.

Why would I give such rigid, negative advice for a feature many consider a bonus to FMP development? (Not to mention risk the ire of so many plugin developers.) There are several reasons:

Clients as a rule do not like plugins. It seems silly that a client might spend $30,000 or $40,000 for database development, and then complain about the cost of one extra copy of FMP or one plugin, but they do. They also gripe about paying for FMP upgrades, and especially plugin upgrades. And they don't quite get it when you explain to them that they need to buy an extra piece of software to make your software work. (They even have difficulty accepting that while they are paying you to provide a FileMaker solution, they must also pay for FileMaker itself.) Selling a client on plugins makes the job just that much more difficult.

Plugins are ephemeral. They come and go and worse, they change. If your solution depends on a plugin that may one day disappear, or become unusable because of an FMP upgrade, you may have a serious problem on your hands.

Many plugins are provided by one-person companies. The chances that these plugins may one day become unavailable are high, and therefore, your chances of embarrassment are high also.

The calling code in plugins may change when the plugin is upgraded. Because some plugins are produced by companies less than adequately concerned with backward compatibility, there is sometimes a loss of compatibility in a new version with previously written calling code. The calling syntax for the plugin has changed. I recall having to rewrite the code in a solution twice because of changes to the syntax of calls made to a single plugin.

Some plugins are very slow. A number of years ago we worked on a pre-existing project that used a popular plugin. The plugin worked exactly as advertised. However, with only a few dozen records in the database, it slowed to a completely unusable crawl. After disconnecting the plugin, the solution zipped right along. Unfortunately, the solution was so inextricably dependant on the plugin, we had to give the client the sad news that a near-complete rewrite was needed. The project ended up being scrapped because of it.

Anyone can write a plugin. Plugins are written by every level of programmer from best to worst. There is always a risk that the plugin you are using was written by someone who never did it before, and did not do an adequate job. You may be risking all your hard work. If you must use a plugin, make certain it is the product of a reputable, qualified programmer.

Free plugins are the biggest risk, but not for the reasons you may think.

Several very well written and reliable plugins are provided free of charge by their authors. However, if you build a solution that relies on a free plugin, you will need that plugin to be available for the lifetime of the solution, and there's the rub.

Free means the author did all that work for nothing; something he is not likely to continue doing. Many of these programmers ask for voluntary donations and with rare exception don't receive a dime. It doesn't take much in the way of disillusionment and disappointment for a programmer to decide either not to continue development of a free plugin, or to stop making it available publicly. If you have to use a free plugin, make sure you write the developer a fat check immediately after he gives you his assurance he will be available to modify the plugin for a fee whenever you might need it. Then be sure to stay in touch with him. You'll need to know how to reach him if he moves.

In the same vein, don't hook your FileMaker database into any other kind of outside software that is likely to become obsolete. "Joe's" word processor, spreadsheet or email client are all out of the question, no matter how much your client insists.

When leveraging plugins, I try to use one from a company that has a long track record and good customer service.

360Works from Atlanta, Georgia and Productive Computing out of southern California, (the evil twins) are both such companies. However, I am not asserting that the plugins from these companies always work perfectly.

In fact, as we mentioned previously, plugins can break due to a wide variety of issues. Breakdowns can come from operating system updates or code changes in the FileMaker platform. The reason I recommend these two companies; is if you call and complain, they will most likely take your complaint seriously and get the issue corrected as soon as possible.

I know this is especially true of 360Works. A verbal conversation with their CEO works wonders in getting bugs fixed in plugins. The one plugin I end up using every single day because I cannot get around it is an HTML email sending plugin from 360Works.

Richard and the "evil twins" (Keith and Mark Larochelle from Productive Computing) at FileMaker DevCon 2017 in Phoenix, AZ.

Richard choking 360Works' CEO, Jesse Barnum, due to a plugin bug.

All smiles after the plugin bug is resolved!

Window Confusion

Take a look at the software products on your hard drive that display multiple open windows. Examine the purposes for those other windows. You will find they generally provide something that is related to the single primary window. They do not compete with it. They augment it, with lists of options, or buttons, or help info, a more detailed view of something contained in the primary window itself, or a separate process (such as a window for composing a letter to a client whose contact information you are viewing in the primary window). These secondary windows never, ever compete with the primary window. They either support it or contain a completely separate process that makes sense in its own secondary window.

If you are uncertain whether or not to create a new window, ask yourself what that new window would look like if you closed the primary window? Could it be mistaken for the primary window? Then don't create it. Use some other device to solve your problem. If a window makes sense with the primary window gone, it probably shouldn't exist.

There are of course exceptions to these rules. With experience you'll know when an exception is indicated. Your clients may for example need to compare two lists of data on the same layout with the data arranged differently in the two windows.

What your users should not be able to do is navigate throughout your system in two or more windows at once. Any secondary window should be limited in its navigation possibilities to layouts that are relevant to the reason for opening the window in the first place. If you have a detail view of a contact open in a secondary window, your users should not be able to get to the system preferences layout in that window. It has nothing to do with a detail view of contact information.

If you determine that you must have two windows open to similar layouts, displaying the same or similar data, dilute the color scheme in the secondary window (make it lighter or more neutral) to visually indicate to the user that it is a secondary window. Never put your user in a situation where he must remember which is the chicken and which the egg.

Make certain the user is not put in a situation where the information in a secondary window (such as a report) is related to some record other than the one he is viewing in the primary window, such that he may lose track of what he was doing and make record changes based on an incorrect recollection.

Additional windows are either directly supportive of the main window, or they are separate processes such as a letter composition view, a report generation view, etc., that do not rely on returning to the same layout in the main window. All windows should make sense and their reason for existence be immediately obvious, all the time.

Even when the reason for opening a secondary window is valid, multiple windows can become problematic. Someone in customer service who needs to be on the phone with multiple clients at once may need to have secondary windows open to detail views for all those contacts. This can lead to clutter and confusion. In such a case it might be better to have a quick jump feature that allows the user to hop back and forth between records, all in a single window, instead of having several windows open at once.

Multiple Files and Data Separation

Every once in awhile you will run into a topic that generates so much angst from developers that you will swear it is a religion. The data separation model is one of the "religions" in the FileMaker community that gets people very excited.

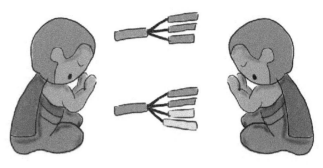

The idea of data separation is that you create one FileMaker file which contains all the user interface and scripts. Then, you relationally connect it to a second FileMaker file which contains all the tables, fields, and data.

The Data Separation Monks

The reason it is discussed and promoted is that a handful of people in the FileMaker community have experience with large data systems where this is a more accepted practice. In large data systems, there sometimes exists an option to put all the user data in one file automatically and have all the coding and structure in a different file.

The "claim-to-fame" for the data separation model is, you can make product changes to the front end file without changing the back end data file. To update a customer solution, all you have to do is swap out the old front end file with the new front end file. That will prevent you from having to reimport all the data that a customer may have cotained in the separate data file.

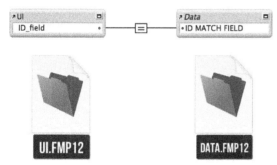

FMI/Apple did not design the FileMaker platform with this separation model in mind. There are FileMaker developers, especially those who make shrink-wrap applications, that swear by this process. At different times, I have worked on projects where we were brought onboard to assist a customer with this sort of setup.

The idea of not having to reimport all of the customer's data is highly appealing. However, the practical execution of this is lacking. What usually ends up happening is you (the developer) end up working on your front end UI file. That is fine. Along the way, you decide to add or edit the structure of the back end data file. What ends up happening is, you have to roll out a new UI file on one side and also roll out a new data file on the back-side. It blows the whole idea of not having to reimport the data.

> **VIDEO TIP - 17 PLATFORM VIDEO COURSE**
> To learn more about the new Data Migration capabilities, check out the 2400 section of videos in the FileMaker 17 video course.

> **FYI**
> Rick Kalman (FileMaker's Director of Product Management and Design) has talked about Future design intentions on the FileMaker Community forum:
>
> http://bit.ly/FMdesignforum17

The whole data separation model and the angst it creates within the community is a symptom of a broader problem. Upgrading and migrating FileMaker solutions has historically sucked. However, starting with the FileMaker 17 release, FMI is actively addressing the simplification of updating and migraing solutions. In the FileMaker 17 release, the FileMaker Data Migration Tool provides a high-speed updated process for deploying a new version of an app that is already in use by users.

In summary, one of the main reasons for using the separation model has been mitigated by the release of the FileMaker Data Migration Tool (FDMT). As a novice or intermediate developer, it is probably in your best interest to keep your FileMaker custom application in a single file. As you become a more senior level FileMaker Jedi, you will find cases where breaking a FileMaker custom application into multiple separate files, can provide performance and scalability benefits. However, this is a very senior conversation and generally not applicable to new or intermediate developers.

Don't "Show Custom Dialog"

FileMaker should be designed in such a way that every time you add the Show Custom Dialog step to one of your scripts, a non-trivial electrical charge goes through your chair.

Here is how to make proper use of this script step:

Pretend it doesn't exist. Then use it only when you can devise no other alternative.

Novices make far too much use of this script step. Custom dialogs should be a rare occurrence in a user's experience. If your users see more than two or three of them in the course of a workday, you probably have too many of them.

Need to ask a user if he wants to print a record to paper or PDF? You could use radio buttons for that, couldn't you? Skip the custom dialog.

Skip them whenever, wherever and however possible. They are for emergencies only. They make the user experience jerky, unprofessional and annoying.

There is another drawback to custom dialogs. Users ignore them and just hit the Enter key. Have you ever installed software on the Windows platform? What do you do? You do what everyone else does; you just keep hitting the Enter key until the software starts to install. You don't actually read those screens. No one does.

The same is true of your database users. They won't read your custom dialog no matter how important it is. They'll just hit the Enter key, assuming that the default choice is the one they want. (Make Cancel the default and they'll be forced to come back and actually read the dialog.)

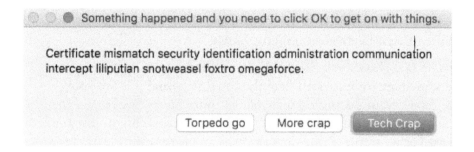

It is more time consuming to write a database in such a way that custom dialogs are seldom required. This is also called the right way!

Title Case and Proper() are Improper

You would think it never occurred to the folks at FMI that FileMaker might be used to create a database with names and addresses in it. Open most any slick contacts database and enter a name in all lower case text. The software will capitalize it for you.

People who use databases absolutely do not want to have to hit that Shift key for every first name and last name they enter; and they shouldn't have to. That's kinda what computers are for, isn't it?

Of course you probably know that FMP has the Title Case style in the Format menu and also the Proper () function, which both do the same thing: set the first letter of each word in a field to upper case and the rest of the word to lower case.

Useless!

These tools won't help people entering data into your solution. They will make it impossible for them. Unless of course your users never ever have to enter a name like McCoy, MacArthur, O'Shea, vanPeebles or any of many other non-conforming names.

If a field is set to use Title Case or the Proper () function, you can try to change Vanpeebles to vanPeebles from now until the end of time and it will never, ever work. FMP will not let you. Your only option is to disconnect these functions and force your users to use the Shift key for every single name and address field in every record ever created.

There have been a couple of possible, though clunky work-arounds, thanks to newer tools available in modern versions of FMP, but they tend to force the user to go back in and retype parts of any name or address that is unusual-Not really the ideal solution.

Another approach used in the past has been to create a lookup table that grabs the correct formatting of names through a relationship. This works, unless the name you need isn't there! It's a dumbed-down solution that is better than nothing. Barely.

This problem leaves you the developer in a bad spot. Computer users are more sophisticated than they used to be and it is not going to escape anyone's attention that your software forces them to use the shift key in every field when other software packages do not. They've all used other software that does the work of proper capitalization for them. Your expensive, custom-built database will seem primitive by comparison. FMI has got to resolve this, but with a twenty+ year history of not resolving this problem, don't hold your breath.

My suggestion is to implement the following auto-enter calculation to the affected text fields:

Case (Exact (Self ; Lower (Self)) ; Proper (Self) ; Self)

You can simply copy and paste the above calc. No field reference is required thanks to the *Self* function, so all fields can use the exact same calc. With this calc in place, whatever a user types into a field will automatically be capitalized with the Proper() function, as long as no upper case letters are present prior to analysis. If there are any upper case letters at all in the typed text, it is an indicaton that the user wants things to be left exactly as typed and therefore the Proper() function is not applied.

The only thing users are required to remember is to use the Shift key only if they want non-standard capitalization, which will usually not be needed.

Since users can readily see when a name/address, etc., is going to require special capitalization treatment, they only have to pay attention to those few field entries involved. Data entry should be fast and easy, requiring no special instruction at all.

Elsewhere in this book I provide a calc for preventing users from inadvertently ruining data integrity by pasting in text from other sources with size/color/ font/ formatting that is unacceptable. Combining the two calcs together, you get this:

TextFormatRemove (Case (Exact (Self ; Lower (Self)) ; Proper (Self) ; Self))

5 Scripts

Allow User Abort

At the beginning of every script you create, the very first step should always be the Allow User Abort step (leave it set it to Off, the default). If this step is not in a script, a user can simply cancel the script in mid-execution and create a genuine mess.

At the very least, it could leave the user on a strange layout from which he cannot escape and at worst, result in data loss or corruption.

If you need a user to be able to abort a script (very unlikely) you can always put in another Allow User Abort step that is set to On at an appropriate point in the script.

There is one gotcha to this advice during development. If you inadvertently write a script in such a way that it gets locked in an infinite loop, you won't be able to get out of it without force-quitting FileMaker. This represents less damage potential in modern versions of FMP than in older versions, but why risk it.

Any time you are working on a script that has a looping routine in it, change the Allow User Abort step temporarily to On until you are finished testing your script and are certain it is bulletproof. If you think circumstances beyond your control might sometimes result in an infinite loop, add a routine to your script that checks the time or some other indicator and drops out of the script gracefully, performing cleanup and housekeeping steps on the way. You never want to allow a user to abort a script or put him in a position of having to force quit FMP.

FYI
Pro Advanced DeBugger can stop a runaway Script.

Don't Use Cut, Copy or Paste in Your Scripts

In the Script Workspace, there are steps available to you that allow you to use your computer's clipboard. These features are largely holdovers from early versions of FileMaker and should no longer be used. If you use these tools in your scripts, sooner or later your user will go to get what they left on the clipboard only to find that something else has mysteriously replaced it. They won't be happy, and by the time the user finally figures out what happened, they will be angry and frustrated when they telephone to call your parentage into question.

If you absolutely must use the clipboard, store what's on there in a global field first and put it back when you're done.

However, even this is not a wise thing to do. When FileMaker was in its infancy, the clipboard was the clipboard, was the clipboard. Period. Today there are a variety of system add-ons that make clipboards hold ten or more different items at once. Chances are good that users will have one of these, and if they have it, they use it. So even if you save and replace the contents of the clipboard you will foul up the location of the other nine items your user was expecting to find where the user left them. The bottom line is: with respect to scripts, the clipboard is out!

My recommendation is to set values into global variables and manage your data with that.

Don't Use AppleScript

I really hate to say this. I love AppleScript. I've done a number of substantial projects in AppleScript and it is a tool that has no equal. In fact, I like AppleScript so much I volunteered a considerable amount of my time with a group of folks who put together much of the documentation that was used to convince Apple not to dicontinue AppleScript when that ridiculous proposal was on the table. Fortunately, Steve Jobs got back into the driver's seat at the right time and all talk of killing off AppleScript ceased.

I never include AppleScript in a FileMaker project and strongly recommend you do not either, though it pains me to do so.

The reason is simple: AppleScript only works on Macs. FMP is a cross-platform environment. Even if you are working in an all-Mac office, sooner or later a Windows machine will be thrown into the mix, or you will decide to make your solution more broadly available. Either way, your AppleScript efforts will be made useless. Whatever you build in FileMaker has to work on both platforms.

Error Trapping in Scripts

This does not refer to the Set Error Capture script step in Script Workspace, but rather to writing your scripts in such a way that users cannot foul them up.

Previously I addressed the Allow User Abort script step and the fact that users must not be allowed to abort a script for fear of causing damage or ending up in the wrong place in your solution. But there are still ways that users can wreak havoc with your solution by way of its scripts.

If your solution has a script that is dependant on the content of a user-accessible feld or user input to perform correctly, all that is needed to confuse or damage your solution is inappropriate or inadequate information provided by the user.

If a script needs to perform a task based on data contained in a field the user has not yet filled out, your script may fail or worse, go into an infinite loop. If your script needs to loop through the records in a portal, but the user hasn't created any yet, your script may fail. There are lots of reasons user input or the lack of it may cause a script to fail: too many to attempt to cover here.

The important point to remember is to look at all the things your script must have in place in order to execute properly, then put routines in your scripts that check for the presence and accuracy of these things before proceeding to any steps that may alter your database. Whenever something is missing or incorrect, throw up a dialog box informing the user of the error, make sure everything is put back the way it was, and then return your user to the layout he started on.

Don't forget to trap for errors you might introduce yourself.

It's all really quite simple: think of everything that might possibly go wrong with a script, however unlikely. Know that it will in fact happen, and head it off in advance. Anticipate.

Halt Script Steps

This is really simple, but it gets absolutely everybody. There are two script steps in ScriptMaker called: Exit Script and Halt Script. These have been badly named since day one. They should be called:

Exit Current Script, and

Stop All Scripts, or something along these lines

The exit script step gets you out of the script you are in, but if the script was called by another script, that script will resume running after the exit script step.

The halt script step gets you completely out of everything. No matter how many subscripts were called to get to the one you're in, everything stops right here at this step.

Here are two dummy script examples:

ScriptOne

Perform Script (ScriptTwo)

Show Custom Dialog ("Hello, glad you're back.")

ScriptTwo

If (Sky = "blue")

    Exit Script

Else

    Halt Script

End If

The first thing ScriptOne does is call ScriptTwo. ScriptTwo decides whether or not the sky is blue. If it is, it will exit (not halt) and the Show Custom Dialog in ScriptOne will give you a polite greeting.

If the sky is not blue, ScriptTwo will halt instead of exit, stopping itself and ScriptOne. All other scripts running will also stop, and you will never see that friendly greeting.

Halt Script is most often used in conjunction with Exit Script in an IF clause just like the ScriptTwo example above to decide whether or not a calling script should continue to run after a subscript has done its work.

Prepare for Upgrades From Day One - Keeping Your Design Structure Consistent

With the release of the FileMaker 17 platform, and the FileMaker Data Migration Tool, the concept of updating users has been radically changed. I highly recommend that you watch the videos in the 2400 section, then potentially revisit this conversation below.

Important Caveat: If the structure and schema of your new FileMaker solution is largely consistent from previous releases, the FileMaker Data Migration Tool will work well for upgrading your users. However, the FDMT fundamentally assumes that the solutions are structurally similar. If you completely alter the table and field structure from one version to the next, the Data Migration Tool will not properly migrate the data.

Obviously, this is completely new territory for the FileMaker community; so best practices for this will evolve over the next several years.

Here is an old school conversation about upgrading and migrating that will be useful if you radically change the design of your custom application:

At some point in creating your database you will decide it is in a useable state and deploy it. You will start entering records, producing reports and in general using the database for the purpose for which you designed it. However, you will also almost certainly continue to improve upon it and at some time will need to replace the version you first deployed with a newer version. It is at this point you will experience a potentially serious problem if upon starting the project you did not create the script(s) recommended here.

Each project should have a script that prepares the database for upgrading to a newer version. We'll call it *PrepareForUpgrade*. Since the older version is the one in use, it is the one containing the records that must be imported into the newer version. Therefore, the very first version of your solution (and all subsequent versions of course) must have this script.

In order for this to work you must have an actual layout for every table in your solution. (Not all tables, such as *Preferences* or *GraphicsStorage* tables, require user layouts and may not already have layouts available. You will have to create some. If you try to rely on a mixture of existing layouts and new layouts created just for upgrading, you end up with an indecipherable jumble.)

The most effective way I have found to make certain this is dealt with correctly from the beginning is to have a set of hidden developer layouts specifically created for and used by your upgrade routines.

I usually name these layouts:

Developer-Upgrade-TableName

or

Maintenance_Upgrade_TableName

This way I can group them together and quickly make certain no tables have been left out.

The script is simple. It freezes the window so the user cannot see what is going on, then goes to each Developer-Upgrade layout in turn where it runs a *Show All Records* script step in each layout. (This is because the import records function of FileMaker will only import records in the current found set(s) of the source file.) The script then goes to the original starting layout and closes the solution.

Be very careful with regard to your shutdown script. Many shutdown scripts are required to perform housekeeping tasks upon shutdown. Some of these might involve find routines that undo what you did with your *PrepareForUpgrade* script. You might need an *If()* clause in your shutdown script that skips some steps if the script sees that it was called from the *PrepareForUpgrade* script.

As long as you have this *PrepareForUpgrade* script in place, none of the problems you may encounter when upgrading your solution are insurmountable.

However allow this to lull you into a false sense of security. Installing an upgrade is at best tedious, and at worse a genuine headache. Do not put off thoughts of designing your upgrade routine. It should be done early on in the development process.

Although you will want to automate the upgrade process as much as possible through scripts, you will still want to take charge of it yourself. No matter how thoroughly you have bulletproofed the process, don't let the client do it, if at all possible.

If you can't do the upgrade on-site, you can probably arrange to do it remotely, or as a last resort, take copies of the client's files to your office and do it there. Remind the client that once you have taken the files, all data subsequently entered will be lost.

First make certain the client's current file(s) is backed up in at least two places, one of which should be offsite. Run the *PrepareForUpgrade* script in the older file. Then move the old database to a different folder, install the new file and run your import script(s).

Note: When designing your import/upgrade routines, it is vital you remember that while the old version was in use, the client was entering new records and incrementing the value of the next number to be entered in all serial number fields. The copy of the database you continued working on does not have all those new records, and therefore will want to enter a much lower number when the next new record is created. Your import scripts must deal with this by getting the highest value for these serial number fields contained in the newly imported records and setting the next serial number to that value plus one. Other similar problems may occur. This is why it is very important that you thoroughly test your upgrade routines before relying on them. Make certain they will work properly by testing with lots of records and under different circumstances. Compare an open copy of the old database with an open copy of the new one, making sure that all related records appear exactly as they should in all layouts. Then, add some new records to make certain none of your portals show related records they should not.

When you are certain the upgrade process has been completed successfully, put the older version in the trash and empty the trash. Then make certain the backups and off-site backups of the older version are out of reach. If you leave the older version anywhere the client has access to it, he will find a way to use it mistakenly. Count on it! Then you will have a real nightmare of a problem to solve.

Lastly, immediately make a backup of the file you have just installed and imported records into, then write the file to a disk and take it back to your office with you as a final precaution.

If you have no choice but to allow your client to install an upgrade on his own, make certain he understands the routine, and that FileMaker Server and all FMP seats have to be shut down first. Make sure the files are all heavily backed up before any upgrade attempt and that your upgrade routines are as user-friendly as possible. Clients will find a way!

Run Script With Full Access Privileges

This one will drive you nuts if you don't know about it. Any time a user runs a script with the "Run script with full access privileges" box checked in Script Workspace, the Get (PrivilegeSetName) function will return [Full Access]. In other words, the feedback you get from FMP is always going to be the Admin's access privileges, which of course will always be the same, [Full Access], regardless of the *actual* user.

Logic would dictate that if you need to use the Get (PrivilegeSetName) function, you want the privilege set name for the current user, not for the temporary circumstances of the script. To get around this *feature*, add a script that calls the script in question, does not have the *Run script with full access privileges* box checked, and which passes your script the user's real privilege set name as a parameter.

Startup & Shutdown Scripts

At the beginning of every project, immediately create both a Startup script and a Shutdown script. Just leave them empty until you know what you want to put in them.

In the File Options dialog of the File menu, set these scripts to be used on startup and shutdown.

It is best to get into the habit of creating these scripts and connecting them right away at the start of every project because you will absolutely, always need them. If you wait to create them later, you'll spend half an hour wondering why your startup and shutdown scripts aren't doing their jobs before you remember that you forgot to connect them.

Startup Scripts are Required; Closing Scripts are Optional

Every client who logs into a FileMaker file is forced to run the established Startup script; the client can't bypass this script. It is not optional.

However, the Close script is optional. Never attach a mission-critical cleanup process to a Close script. Many users just close laptops or shut off mobile devices in the middle of using FileMaker.

If I had to guess, I would say half of mobile users never quit FileMaker the correct way. Their devices simply go to sleep, and the FileMaker Server gracefully disconnects them. The Close script is not run during that disconnection process. If you have mission-critical items that run in the Close script, you should expect that half of your users will never actually run that script.

Robots

Depending upon the needs of your customer, you may have some time-consuming scripts that need to run for a variety of reasons. As previously mentioned in this book, scripts can do all sorts of work to make your life better. You can certainly use scripts to pre-cache reports, so they are displayed quickly for a customer. Some reports have a lot of calculations and displaying them will take time. As we covered, you can pre-cache this information into text and number fields, so the reports are displayed rapidly.

Fairly small scripts can be run in a Startup script if they do not take a lot of time. If it takes more than five to ten seconds to run, then you should consider setting up a robot for the customer.

A robot is a Mac or Windows machine that is ideally on the same network as the FileMaker server. This Mac or Windows computer is not used by anyone; for any other purpose. Its sole job is to run scripts on some schedule. Notice the example below; this robot runs on an RCC network. There is a simple ListView that shows the time's specific scripts will be executed.

Also, to prevent crashing on the client, the FileMaker database quits around midnight and reopens itself within the hour, as part of a scripted schedule for the operating system. By quitting and re-opening FileMaker, any weird memory leaks will be cleared out.

Note: The Robot we are discussing in this section is YOUR Mac or Windows Computer Running FileMaker Pro. FMI, also has a hidden process that runs on the FileMaker Cloud called "FileMaker Cloud virtual DBA bot." This is the actual FMC process that tries to complete the middle of the night maintenance. Watch out for the confusing terminology.

FYI

If you are using FileMaker Cloud then you want your robot to be an (AWS) Amazon EC2 server that runs in the same region as where your FileMaker Cloud is installed.

A robot connected to a database on FMC, should always be shut down from 12am-3am.

TERMINOLOGY

Memory leaks are a defect in the programming of any application. This can happen to plugins or to FileMaker clients if FMI makes a coding mistake in the application. You can run into situations where the client will run for months at a time with no problems. Or it will not run more than two to three days without crashing. A daily restart of the FileMaker Pro application may be useful.

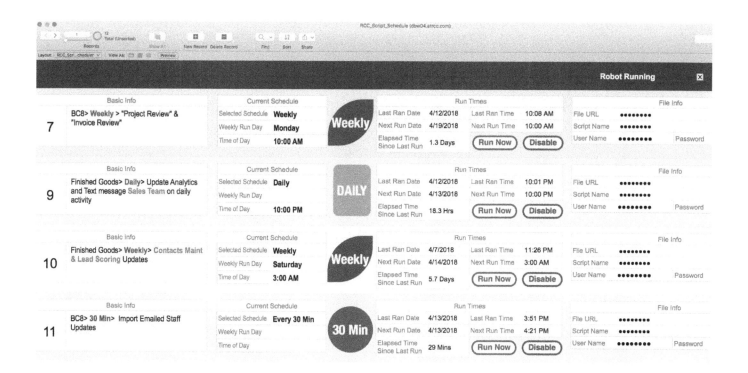

> **TERMINOLOGY**
>
> SASE stands for Server Assisted Script Execution. This is not an official FMI endorsed term.
>
> PSOS stands for Perform Script on Server.

> **FYI**
>
> PSOS and SASE both leverage a hidden copy of FileMaker Pro. This is completely headless, with no visual display.

Some people think that running a scheduled script on a FileMaker Server is the way to go. However, using SASE to run scheduled scripts on a FM Server can be bad.

Why?

Essentially, FileMaker Server has an invisible copy of FileMaker Pro that runs under-the-hood. When this client is activated, FileMaker Server sees this client as a separate process and treats it as a separate logged-in client (this is cool).

The issue is that this client is headless (i.e., there is no visual indication as to what the invisible client is doing). If you run a script on your copy of FileMaker Pro, you can visually see what is happening. When SASE runs, there is absolutely no visual indication of what it is doing or where it may be having a problem.

Another problem is that the client is "on" the FileMaker Server. If the SASE process fails, the odds are that people who need to be notified of this, will not receive any email notifications. It is easy for a script to be set up on a FileMaker Server to run with SASE, and for everyone to forget about it. Then, people wonder why specific reports or other functionalities in their database seem broken.

With SASE, if the script is too big, unwieldy, and takes a long time to run, it could crash the FileMaker client that is running on the server. Remember, the SASE process is separate from the core server process. That means if the SASE process crashes or stops working, the FileMaker Server process will keep running. Because of this, a SASE crash will be invisible to most everyone. You may not receive an email notification about it, for a wide variety of reasons.

Restarting the server may be required to fix this process. That means taking the whole server offline and potential downtime.

Taking the SASE process and running it on FileMaker Pro is a bit more expensive (since you have to buy another Mac or Windows computer). However, since the process is running in Pro, you can provide some parental supervision by watching the scripts run.

Consider putting a monitor on the machine and have it running in the office, so you can visually keep an eye on it. If it does something crazy or unexpected, someone can make a note that the robot has gone berserk.

If FileMaker Pro crashed for some reason, then

    A) You will see it crash

    and

    B) Remember, FileMaker Pro is expected to crash, and the FileMaker Server will deal with the crash very gracefully. Having the built-in SASE client crash is unexpected, and the FileMaker Server does not deal with that gracefully.

What RCC's Robot does for us over the course of the day:

1) Updates our lead scoring reports (daily), in terms of tracking our customers and audiences activities with RCC.

2) Performs maintenance and reporting (daily) on Staff metrics and caches data into the Daily Analytics table.

3) Talks to PayPal (hourly) to determine if any Invoices have been paid. Then, it emails the client and messages the engineer to inform them an Invoice was paid.

4) Sends out text messages (nightly) to senior management about specific metrics that are in a parameter, in terms of Staffing.

5) Sends out staff performance reports (weekly) via pdf and email. These reports take a lot of calculation processing and have various charting images embedded. It generates a PDF for each Staff member and emails the PDF to each person.

6) Because of the large volume of people that subscribe to RCC's videos, some of the processing takes several hours to complete. So as the process runs, it creates a log entry of the beginning and ending time of each activity.

6 Dealing With Clients

Always Give Them More Than They Expect

This is just common business sense, but is relevant and somewhat contradictory to some sections. It is also distinctly more possible in the profession of FMP development than in many others.

First off, it is hard to be generous if you happen to feel you're working on the cheap. Never, ever discount your work. If your rate is $100 an hour and a client wants you to work for $75, refuse the project. A discounted hourly rate is not better than nothing, because you will feel bitter and resentful through the whole project and will not do your best work. It's just human nature. You won't intentionally do less than your best, you just will.

Clients who want a discount usually want to shave hours too. You'll end up working for $50 an hour. And never agree to a lower rate, then charge more hours than you've actually worked to make up the difference. In this business, your integrity is everything. Clients must know they can trust you absolutely and word travels fast.

Charge your full-boat rates all the time, to everyone, no exceptions. Then you won't be resentful or bitter, and oddly, your clients will respect you more. You'll feel well compensated and will want to give your clients that little extra that makes them even more appreciative of your work.

Clients are like any other group. They range from the intolerable to the delightful. When I first wrote this quite a few years ago, I happened to have been working for a client who falls into the latter category; she was a joy to work for and I gave her tons of extras just because I liked working for her so much. Relish this when you get it, it is somewhat rare.

If you are not getting short-changed on your hourly rate you can afford to, and will want to give something extra to most all your clients, even those who don't fall into your favorites category. The more enjoyable, the more you'll want to give them.

People generally do not feel they have gotten their money's worth if they get only what they paid for. This is simple human nature. They won't feel cheated, but they won't feel grateful either. If a client gets exactly what he asked and paid for, he'll be happy with his purchase but he won't brag about you to his friends and colleagues.

If you purchase a new TV set and a smiling clerk takes your money and hands you the box, you'll probably be happy with the purchase but you won't give that clerk another thought. Any clerk will do in the future. If on the other hand he says, "this box is pretty heavy, let me take it to your car for you" him you'll remember!

Do the same for your clients. Don't just deliver what they asked for. Take it to the car for them.

If you work eight hours in a day but feel you've only accomplished the equivalent of five hours of quality work, send your client a time slip that shows the full eight hours, but also shows that you are billing him for only five and *tell him* (it means nothing if he doesn't know about it) why you cut your own bill. On an especially off day, you may want to tell your client you worked all day and got nowhere, no charge. If you're really on fire a particular day and feel you did twelve hours of work in only six, tell him that too (just don't charge for twelve hours).

If you happen to think of a fantastic new feature not in the design specs but one that you feel would greatly benefit your client, put it in and don't charge him for it (again, be sure to tell him about it). I will usually say something like; "Hey, I had a great idea for a new feature. It took a few hours and I know you didn't ask for it, but I just had to put it in for you. I'll take it out if you don't like it. No charge either way."

There is a bonus to giving clients free features. If you do, when they come to you with a feature request (see *feature creep* pg. 105) that you feel is unreasonable, they won't be as likely to get upset when you tell them you have to charge extra for it or that you don't want to do it.

If you have to learn a new technique for your project, tell your client how much time you spent getting up to speed and be sure they know you're not charging for that time (don't mention this if it is a case where it is reasonable to assume you should have already possessed that knowledge).

I often get asked to analyze existing projects. I have the client send me the project and a retainer check (usually for 5-10 hours). If the project is particularly bad and therefore I didn't have to spend more than an hour or two looking at it in order to come up with the bad news, I'll tell them something like; "Look, I'm not going to charge you for this. It is bad enough to have to hear this news, I'm not going to pour salt into the wound by billing you for it too. The full amount of your retainer is still available."

I also get occasional requests for minor new features in existing databases someone else developed. If the database is reasonably well structured and the request is only a few minutes work, I'll sometimes simply institute the change(s), or tell them how to do it themselves, and tell the client "no charge". If you think about it, this not only creates good will, but also saves you work. You don't want to take the time to set up an account for a client who needs just ten minutes of work. And you don't want to ask a client to send you a retainer he won't use. If it's fast and easy, give it away. You *will* get it back.

There are lots of things you can do to make clients believe they got more than they paid for. If you feel you're getting adequately compensated, this is easy to do and a great habit to develop. Your clients will be grateful, will brag about you to their friends, and in the bargain, you'll feel good too.

There is one gotcha to avoid here: *developer feature creep*. Be careful not to be too generous with free added features. They can (a) convince your client that feature creep is OK and (b), if you get too carried away, you can make development run past the projected completion time, or even paint yourself into a corner.

Communicate With Your Client

OK, so this doesn't have much to do with software design, but it does have to do with keeping your client informed and happy, which will allow you to continue working on his project. Fail to do this and you may have no project to worry about designing.

- *Send your client a daily time slip (email works best) showing what hours you worked and what you did during those hours.*

- *Send your client a weekly report on the number of hours used during that week, and highlighting the major changes/additions made. Since he can't see you working, he will assume you are not working unless he can see what work has been done and what progress is being made.*

- *Have a review conference with the client at least once a week (over the internet using voice and screen sharing software) to show him the latest build, go over what has been done and what needs to be done next, and to get his input.*

- *Zip and email the client every build as soon as it is done. If important new features have been added, or you have just begun a new aspect of the project, this is a good time for a review. This is not necessary if the database is running on a FileMaker Server with good backups.*

- *Take notes of every communication and contact with the client. You will be surprised just how often a client tells you he did or didn't ask for something when the opposite is true. You will forget things also. Write it down. Plus, clients tend to get pissed if they are talking and you are not writing. I understand and appreciate this. I have had staff in meetings, who were not visibly scribbling down notes; so the clients call and yell at me. When interrogating my staff, they claimed that the information provided to them was trivial and not worth writing down. I explained to them that this was not a negotiation; they had to do it.*

Don't Let the Client Design the Project

Nothing will lead to a badly designed software project faster than a client who thinks he knows how the system should be designed and insists you do it his way. This will happen more often than you might think.

You will, from time to time, get a client who has read the FileMaker manual, or worse, dabbled a little with building a database. I had one such client long ago who referred to absolutely everything in FileMaker as a relationship. It was impossible to understand what he wanted, because he called every field, layout, script and table a relationship. I often asked him to stop using jargon and speak to me in plain English, but he continued to say relationship a dozen times per phone call. I think the only time he didn't use the term was when he was actually talking about a relationship!

The worst thing you can do is to build a database the way your client thinks it should be done. At the same time, you might find it difficult to convince him to just tell you what he needs and leave the how up to you. In these cases, separate his needs from the way he believes it should be done, then do it the right way. You may have to disguise the solution to make it look as if it were built the way he wanted, but you'll be better off than if you follow his plan. A few dummy fields sprinkled here and there will usually do the trick. (I have another client who to this day believes a primary key field designed his way actually does something. It doesn't.) Yes, this is deceitful. But it will get you in far less trouble than building a project in a manner that is unworkable. Your only other option with an obstinate client is to turn down the project.

All that said, keep in mind that your client should have a very detailed understanding of their business processes and should be able to communicate these to you efficiently. Additionally, the client may have ideas on how the layout might be structured or how the solution might work from an interface standpoint.

It is super useful to listen to these ideas and to incorporate them as often as possible. If the customer insists on telling you how to structure the underlying custom solution, then you need to be very careful. We have also had clients dictate to us the number of hours a block of development should take to create. I know this sounds strange, but I had someone who was not a coder telling me exactly how long the development should take. I suspect that their cousin Vinny said to them that it would take X number of hours. Neither one of them were professional FileMaker developers. We fired this client shortly after that.

Along these same lines, make certain your client understands that you will refuse to work for him if he insists on dabbling with the database himself. Before you deliver a project, make a record of the number of fields, tables, value lists, etc., in case you may need to check for this. Some clients will alter the solution and not tell you about it.

Just as with backup schemes, if the client pushes you to use an inadequate design, or accept his dabbling with the solution, the disastrous end result is *your* fault. He will see it that way, and he will be right.

Feature Creep

When you are half way through a project and the client calls you to ask, *can you make it do this too*? That is *feature creep*: the addition of new features or functionality not included in the original design specifications.

There is another term for feature creep... *project cyanide*! Taken in not very large doses, it can be fatal. At the very least, it will make you sick.

First, you should know that all projects suffer from at least attempted, feature creep. I can't think of a single project I've ever done where I didn't get at least one call mid-project, asking for new functionality. This is one of the many important reasons for having all that documentation mentioned before.

If you do not have the aforementioned documents, all features are original design specifications. You can't refuse any requests because all requests are, by definition, part of the original design (because you don't have one!).

If you're getting paid by the hour (and you should be), then feature creep might not sound like such a bad thing. A new feature means more work and therefore more money. No one objects to more money. But a new feature, if substantial enough, may just invalidate your basic design concept, forcing you to start over if you want to add the feature.

More subtly, a new feature can trickle through your system, breaking code you've already finished and forcing you to rewrite complex routines.

Ideally, all of the design documents are *sign-off documents*. That is, the client should sign each document indicating that he/she agrees it is an exact and complete description of how things are or what they want, expect and have agreed to. If it's not in the documentation then it's not part of the project. This helps to stave off the poisonous effects of feature creep.

However, a client who is requesting an additional feature is not being unreasonable (at least not from his viewpoint) and you can't be unreasonable either. Simply telling clients *it's not in the design specs and therefore I won't do it* won't make you a lot of friends. You can't reject requests out-of-hand, even ones that happen to be ridiculous, but you also can't accept requests that would result in disaster for the project.

In the interest of the success of your project, you must keep feature creep at bay as much as humanly possible. Your response to a mid-project request should roughly take the form of one of the examples below (assuming you have a design specifications document, without which you are on your own and captain of a sinking ship):

- *"I can add that feature for you right away. It will only take me a few minutes, won't interfere with the existing code and is a great idea. In fact, I've already implemented it for you while we've been talking on the phone."*

- *"I can add that feature for you. It is not in the design specifications and will take XX additional hours beyond the original estimate at a cost of YY additional dollars and will have ZZ limitations. Do you want me to go ahead with it?"*

- *"I can add that feature for you. However, it is not in the design specifications and because of the complexity of the new feature will require rewriting a substantial amount of the code already in place. This will take XX additional hours beyond the original estimate at a cost of YY additional dollars and will have ZZ limitations. Do you want me to go ahead with it?"*

- *"It is possible to implement this functionality. However, it is not in the design specifications and affects the project design at a sufficiently fundamental level that it would be necessary to redesign the project and start coding from scratch. Do you want me to start the project over from the beginning?"*

- *"Your feature request is a nice idea, but is not part of the design specifications and is impractical from a technical standpoint. It would be too prone to failure if it worked at all, and I fervently advise against it. In fact, reluctantly I feel I must refuse this request."*

- *"Your request is a good idea, but it is not in the current design specifications, would take XX additional hours beyond the original estimate at a cost of YY additional dollars, and would push back our completion date. I think it would be wise to add this to the feature list for the next version of the software, rather than attempting to include it now."*

- *"I never created a design specifications document, therefore this request holds exactly the same weight as all the other requests you've made and I have no grounds on which to reject it. I don't know if it will interfere with the overall design because I don't have one, don't know how much extra it will cost because I never created a cost estimate, and can't say if it will bring down the technical structure because I don't have a plan for that either… sure, I'll do it!"*

(Sorry, I couldn't resist that last one. It just seemed too funny at the time.)

Give Them What They Need, Not What They Want

The title sounds quite flippant, but this concept is very important and applies equally whether you are building a solution for a client or for yourself. Exactly the same kind and severity of errors can be made in either case. It is doubly difficult to avoid these errors if *you* are the client because it is more difficult to maintain sufficient distance from the project for a healthy impartiality and to make the necessary judgments and decisions.

Every project begins at the same place: the client telling you what he/she wants. Novice developers all make exactly the same mistake at this point and it is very often fatal.

What the client wants is, with rare exception, not what the client needs! Rushing ahead and simply building what the client asked for is virtually guaranteed to lead to a failed project. (Some clients will insist on this and it is better to simply pass on these projects.)

Imagine you are a doctor. A patient comes to you and says, *I need my appendix removed; it hurts*. Taking at face value what a client says he wants and proceeding to build a solution based on that statement is exactly the same as wheeling your patient straight to surgery and removing his appendix on his say-so.

Baaaaaad idea!

When you take on a client you have an obligation to that client (and for the sake of self-preservation) to determine what he really needs as opposed to what he believes he needs. *You* are the expert. Therefore, you must determine what is needed. Always.

I need my appendix removed; it hurts, really means *I have a pain in my belly, please make it go away*. In order to fulfill your professional obligations, you must take a case history, examine the patient, make a diagnosis and determine a course of treatment, while largely ignoring the reference to the appendix. Otherwise you are guilty of malpractice.

In order not to be guilty of malpractice as a database developer, you must:

- *Understand in detail how things are currently done in your client's business. Follow and document all relevant workflows from beginning to end.*

- *Determine what you think your client needs based on interviews with your client and his staff; on your observations of day-to-day work performed; and on employee descriptions of what they believe they need; on where work runs into bottlenecks, and on what they would like to be able to do that they cannot currently do. (Remember, statements about how work is performed may often differ from what you observe.)*

- *Ignore what the client initially said he needed. Determine on your own what he needs. Then revisit his statement of what he needs in light of your findings.*

- *Based on the foregoing, determine what software solution needs to be built and what must be the central theme of the solution.*

- *Determine what technical approach and techniques are required to build the solution.*

All of the foregoing is done on paper in the form of an *existing system document*, a *requirements analysis document*, a *design specifications document* and a *technical specifications document*. These are your case history, examination, diagnosis and treatment plan. If you don't have them, you cannot possibly provide the correct solution to your client's problems, because you would instead be building a solution based on a layman's description of his needs.

Always remember, when a client says, *please build me XYZ*, you should always hear *please find out what I need and build that for me*. Never just build *XYZ*.

YODA SAYS

Gain more experience, better you will be, "see" the client needs you will.

Instinctual skill set you will have, trouble you will sense. Feel like a Jedi you will. (as if Richard knows what a Jedi skill feels like). LOL!

Clients Should Never Look Over Your Shoulder

In previous versions of this book, I made the case that clients should never watch you build a FileMaker solution. I have moderated my tone on this. These days, I can also make a case for when it is highly beneficial for a user to watch you build a FileMaker solution.

But, it depends on the developer's personal preferences, their technical skills, and their self-confidence. If you are still learning and do not feel like you have a ninja-level grasp of FileMaker, then having the customer watch you is probably not a great thing.

However, we have run into situations where customers who are paying for development do not appreciate the work and effort that goes into it. We do not need a parade where the customer sings how wonderful and awesome we are. However, if a customer does not appreciate what you have done, they will frequently bitch and whine about the bill. They may complain about what they are paying, even if you are under-budget.

The fundamental issue, as a general rule is, people do not understand the software development process, period. In fact, if you were an expert in the software development process, you would not be reading this book. We all have to start somewhere.

There will be times when it is beneficial to let the customer watch over your shoulder. If they suddenly say, "Well, that's a simple change to make." and you know that it will take all day to make the change, you might want to invite them to watch.

In fact, sometimes it is good for the customer to learn some basic FileMaker skills; so they can help maintain their solution going forward. This depends on your overall philosophy of the FileMaker solution. If you believe that FileMaker is a special tool that only properly trained developers should use, then lock the customer out of the application and never let them see you use it.

Some developers prefer their customers have minimal skills; so they can help support themselves. My philosophy is that the developer is needed only when serious heavy-duty development work is required.

There are times when having the customer watch and be provided with training while doing the development is beneficial. Keep in mind; this will double or triple the time it takes to build a given block of functionality. This extra time has to be calculated upfront as part of your budget conversation with the customer.

The Client is Always Wrong

Well, not really, but it was a cute title. You will not be called upon to build a completely new solution nearly as often as you will be asked to work on an existing solution. This makes perfect sense. FileMaker has been around for decades, so there are more solutions already out there than new ones currently needed.

Ninety-nine percent of the time, the existing solution you are asked to work on will be a mess. After all, if the solution were a properly built, professional job the client would probably be calling the person who built it, not you.

The request you will get from the client will almost certainly be to add a new feature or repair some existing feature that no longer works. This is what the client believes he needs, but it is seldom what is actually needed, hence the title.

When you open the file(s) you are likely as not going to find an unworkable solution. Something cobbled together with little rhyme or reason and impossible to work with. As has happened to me quite a few times, you may find that what the client wants is simply not possible or practical with the current design or lack of it in his database.

Now you face a difficult problem. Do you tell the client his database is trash, or keep quiet? Keeping quiet is a tacit agreement to do the work requested. If the database is bad enough, your additions/changes won't work properly and you'll get the blame deservedly so.

If you tell the client his database is junk, chances are, you're going to upset him. If he didn't already know it was junk, he'll suspect you of ulterior motives. If he did already know, he'll still be upset because he was hoping you'd tell him otherwise. This is a tread-lightly, seldom-win situation that requires your very best diplomacy. You must tell the client the truth and you have to find a way to do it that is palatable or you'll simply lose the client. Don't ask me how to approach this. I still wing it every time. You're on your own. But there's another common zinger involved here that you'd better know about or you'll lose a lot of these clients that you could have saved.

Look at the situation from the client's point of view. Usually he knows nothing about FileMaker. All he does know is that he paid a lot of money (it's always a lot of money — I swear, if they spent $1.85 on the whole project, they'd call it *a lot of money*) for a solution that doesn't work properly and now he's discovered, thanks to you, that it can't be made to work properly. He's liable to remark, or at least think; *This FileMaker thing is crap!*

Stop and read that again. What's happening here? This is extremely important. Did you get it?

Clients by and large do not distinguish between FileMaker Pro and the solutions built in it! They believe that the crappy solution they are looking at *is* FileMaker Pro. Good luck getting them to understand that FileMaker is just a tool and that their previous developer used a *good tool* to build a *lousy solution*. Every time they open their solution they see FileMaker Pro emblazoned everywhere. You are not going to get through to them that FileMaker and their current solution are not one and the same thing. Their logic is as follows:

- *Solution = crap*
- *Solution = FileMaker*
- *FileMaker = crap*
- *You = Another FileMaker developer*
- *Another FMP developer = another crappy solution*

That logical progression takes the client about one millisecond (if you watch carefully, you can see this data exchange take place in his eyes - it's a lightning-fast ripple that is gone in an instant), and you're dead before you hit the ground.

Here's where I ride in on my white horse and come to your rescue! (You're welcome.)

You can actually win this scenario almost every single time, if you come prepared. Since you know you're going to tell the client his solution is garbage and that he needs to pay you to build a new one, there is no excuse for not being properly equipped.

Choose the slickest most visually awe-inspiring solution you've built, that you can show off without compromising an NDA. If you don't have anything, build one. It's worth the effort because this package will make you a lot of money.

Remember what I said previously about a good-looking solution with bad code selling better than a bad looking solution with great code? This is where that bit of information really comes in handy.

Your demo solution doesn't have to do much. It just has to look fantastic. Pick something that looks gorgeous on both Windows and Macintosh and build a stand-alone version for each platform so you don't have to worry whether or not clients have the right version of FMP installed on any specific machine.

If you do not have anything ready to go, then feel free to download a copy of FM Starting Point as an example of awesome stuff that you can build in FileMaker. Yes, we both know that this is not your solution, but I am trying to help you be successful as a FileMaker developer. Just remember that you owe me your firstborn child or your favorite cat, if you have one.

When you know you are going to drop a bombshell on your client regarding his awful existing solution, start with: *I'd like to show you something.* Don't say anything about FileMaker. Disguise the fact that it is a FileMaker solution as much as you can. Just install your solution and run it for him. Show off all the bells and whistles.

If you show them FM Starting Point, tell them that this is a free solution they can use to start their next project, it will save them a ton of time and money.

When you think they are sufficiently impressed, start up their old solution and show them the two solutions side-by-side. Explain to them that your slick solution was built in FileMaker Pro, just like their crappy one. Then let this information sink in for a minute. If you see that lightning-fast ripple in their eyes again, you know you're home free. At the very least, they are not likely to continue thinking that FileMaker Pro is the problem.

Now that they get it, it's safer to deliver the bad news about their existing terrible solution. Just tell them that their database looks just as bad behind the scenes as it does visually on the screen and that it has nothing to do with FileMaker but rather with the person who built their solution. Now it will make sense. From there it will be a snap to explain to them that the work they requested is not really the problem, and that it can't be done in the current solution.

If you have read this section and you truly understand and follow it, then you know how excellent this advice is. I am pretty sure whatever you paid for this book, it is not enough. Feel free to drop me a note or a short video about how awesome FM Starting Point is or how much you enjoyed this book.

> **THE MORE YOU KNOW**
>
> A number of top-shelf FileMaker consultancies use FM Starting Point when first meeting customers, in an effort to get their business. I have personally had to compete against other consultancies who used FM Starting Point (RCC's software) as part of their quote. When I see this happen, I just laugh. Of course it is up to the customer to decide which consultant they will work better with.

Think Like a Spy

OK, you won't need a pistol or a secret decoder ring, but you do have to be security minded if you develop databases for anyone other than yourself. If you are developing a database for a client then you will be in possession of:

- *Their source code (after all, you're writing it)*
- *Their secret company data (at least some of it)*
- *All their passwords*
- *A responsibility to see to it that it is impossible for anyone to get these things away from you*
- *Not nearly enough money to cover the law suit that will surely follow if you don't fulfill the preceding obligations*

Here is more spy stuff to do:

- *Consider using EAR (Encryption At Rest) with the customer's database. This is a bit tedious, but modern encryption algorithms are so sophisticated, no one is going to be able to hack in.*
- *Have a password-protected screen saver.*
- *Keep your office door locked at all times.*
- *Work behind a bulletproof firewall. Some pimply-faced teenager with nothing to do is just itching to get into your system: don't let him. One of the best things you can do to prevent this, aside from the firewall, is to make sure your most exposed machine is a Mac and any other computers on the network are on a secondary intranet. All those zit-covered teenagers focus their efforts on the Windows platform which they can often successfully break into. Fortunately, they don't consider the Mac to be worth the effort.*
- *Do not talk about your clients in public. Your client may consider the fact that you are working for him to be a secret, and it is just not good policy to blab about clients. Keep it to yourself.*
- *Give your client a non-disclosure agreement. Don't wait for him to ask for it. Offer it without being asked. Stick to it religiously. In fact, interpret it more broadly than you think necessary. Your clients will notice and appreciate that you are so cautious with their information.*
- *Do not use any of your clients as a reference unless you have permission to do so.*
- *Likewise, do not show any project you have done for a previous client to a prospective client, unless you have permission to do so.*

TERMINOLOGY

FMI does not call EAR, "EAR". They call it "database encryption." The problem is that this is an imprecise term, since there are at least three types of encryption in the FileMaker platform. For example, there is SSL encryption, which is encrypting the data as it transfers over the network. There is also field-level encryption.

So "database encryption" is way too vague for me to use. However, I have seen them use that term on the certification test, so watch out!

VIDEO TIP - 17 PLATFORM VIDEO COURSE

To learn more about "EAR" (Encryption at Rest) watch video "1205 - Encryption at Rest (EAR)".

Store Client Passwords in Three Places

Your client will lose his master password (and very often change it first, without telling you). Store his master password in at least three different places both in your office and off-site. You *will* need it.

Hacking the Password in FileMaker

The reality is that FileMaker is a very secure platform. If someone is using EAR encryption on a FileMaker file and the passwords are lost, there is absolutely no method of recovery, short of some level of effort by the NSA to crack your software.

If the password does not have EAR encryption enabled, then it is possible to hack your way into the file, if you have physical possession of the file (i.e., you have the .fmp12 file on your hard drive). It is impossible to remote hack a FileMaker file with any known technique.

TERMINOLOGY

Notice again that I am not using "database encryption", which is a vague term. I am specifically identifying a particular area of encryption.

There is third-party software which can go into a FileMaker file and add an administrative level access code to the file. Again, this will only work if the file does not have EAR encryption enabled. The password hacking tool will not tell you any of the previous passwords. It just gives you a brand new password that allows you to access the file as an administrator.

This third-party software is not recommended or authorized in any way by FMI. It is a real tool that exists on the internet, and it is pretty inexpensive.

If you are a serious FileMaker developer, you need to know about this. Knowing this tool exists, easily makes the case that you should be using EAR encryption to protect your FileMaker application.

Remember, this tool only works if the person has the FileMaker file on their hard drive. Having remote access, over the internet, will not cut it.

7 Don't Abuse FileMaker

Client File Integrity

As we discuss in other areas of this book, if you are hired to work on a customer project, there is probably a 50/50 chance that you will be working on an existing FileMaker file.

When you walk into this situation, you are hoping that the file is well commented, well designed, etc. But other issues can creep into your project.

It is possible to abuse FileMaker to the point that it will not open or run any further. As a novice, it is probably unlikely you have seen this. But it can and will happen, and it freaks everyone out when it does.

If the FileMaker file runs a customer business (i.e., it is "Mission Critical") and it suddenly will not open, the customer (if they have a brain) will panic. Hopefully, they will not blame you for this. However, if this happens "on your watch," then the customer will blame you. Not good.

If you are planning on working in the FileMaker business, then this will eventually happen to you. Expect it to happen. How do you keep this from being a disaster? You need two techniques.

(1) Mitigate the issue by limiting the chances of a file becoming corrupted.

(2) Know the emergency procedures for when this happens.

"Mitigate the issue" means take good care of a FileMaker file and not abuse it. FileMaker abuse primarily comes from a customer using a previously crashed FileMaker file. How can this happen?

Abuse comes from NOT closing a FileMaker file properly. That means the file is running (on Pro or Server) and the app crashes. If the FileMaker database application crashes, then it was NOT properly closed down.

Below are some common situations:

(A) A user is running a .fmp12 file locally on their computer and FileMaker Pro crashes. Then this person re-opens and uses the file that crashed. Very Bad. Always restore from the last good backup. Did this user make a backup in the last hour or two??? No??? Then they should be running the file on FileMaker Server, and the server should be running backups every hour (or maybe even every 15 minutes).

(B) FileMaker Server crashes, and the Server admin (the person who babysits the server) restarts the server and has utilized the previously crashed file. The "safe play" is always to assume that a "crashed file" has been "damaged." In reality, it may or may not have been damaged. In general, there is NO way to be sure. So why risk it??? Please do not!!!

Important Note: If a file is running on FileMaker Server or FileMaker Cloud, and a client crashes, the .fmp12 file is protected from damage by the Server, which is still running normally. The Server "sees" that the client has disappeared, and it logs the clients out without damaging the file.

My life is considerably simpler after making the decision to NEVER use a crashed file. My team typically manages forty or fifty FileMaker Servers. Within the past five years, I have only seen one file magically get corrupted, due to unknown means. This was a legit corruption. NOT connected to a crash. So out of five hundred or more files, only one got hosed. Did I panic? No! We restored a backup from two days prior - to use a clean file. The customer was happy to re-enter the data, as opposed to permanently losing the whole file.

The moral of the story is: always take good care of your file, and be on the lookout for other users abusing their files. If you know a customer has been abusing their file, I would seriously recommend you eject from the project before getting in too deep. The exception is if you have had a detailed conversation with the customer, and they understand that your job is to rebuild the file from scratch.

Is this "corruption stuff" really this bad? Maybe not. However, you really cannot tell. This is like driving home 90 MPH on the freeway. If you do it once, will you get a ticket from the police? Probably not. What if you do it every day for a month? You are going to get busted by the cops. It only takes ONE time to get a ticket.

Do you feel lucky???

Clients Will Not Perform Backups

A backup system is an integral part of your software design. Don't overlook it, but also don't count on it.

There are some very stubborn clients out there who will steadfastly refuse to follow your advice, and who will then blame you when everything blows up in their faces.

Rule # 1 — *All* databases suffer an unrecoverable crash sooner or later

Rule # 2 — *All* unrecoverable crashed databases are your fault

Unrecoverable databases are your fault because you did not make certain there was a backup system in place that the client could not turn off, foul up, or otherwise interfere with.

Carve this in stone:

- *Your client will ignore your backup admonitions*
- *Your client will interfere with your backup system*
- *Your client will foul up your backup system*
- *Your client will turn off your backup system*

You can count on these things exactly as much as you can count on the sun rising in the morning.

Think of it in the same terms as defensive driving. Assume the other fellow is going to always do the stupidest thing possible under the circumstances and plan ahead for it. If you put a backup system into place that requires a client to do nothing more than push a button to make backups, he won't do it!

Written guarantees available in the lobby.

Find an automated backup scheme (FileMaker Server is indispensable for this) that fits your client's situation the best and implement it. Make certain there is off-site backup as well (fires and robberies happen). The greater the rate of data entry, the more frequently backups should take place. Make certain your client always keeps the last several weeks of hard copy data because under some circumstances manual re-entry of data may be the only option. Check frequently to be certain backups are actually taking place and are stored everywhere necessary.

FileMaker Cloud backs up automatically every twenty minutes and is not something that the client can monkey with. FileMaker Cloud also runs a maintenance process every night, sometime between midnight and 3 am. The time is local to wherever the server is at. During this maintenance process, one additional backup is created and automatically preserved. A preserved backup is never scheduled for deletion or removal. There are customers who have run FileMaker Cloud successfully for more than a year, and they end up with more than 365 backups. The downside to this is that they will probably pay an additional $10-20/month. The upside is that they have good backups that go for a long time.

Of course, you can manually log into the FileMaker Cloud Admin Console and tell the console to delete specific backups.

Database Backup Strategy - FileMaker Cloud

One of the most critical parts of learning the FileMaker platform is this whole section on data integrity. The idea of "not abusing the FileMaker file," fundamentally depends upon not utilizing a previously crashed file. But this depends upon having a fresh backup that you can use. Otherwise, you will be using a crashed backup.

So what should the backup schedule be?

The backup schedules in FileMaker Cloud are not manually configurable. As mentioned above, the backups on FileMaker Cloud run automatically every 20 minutes and are preserved for seven days. A second backup schedule attempts to run daily, some times between 12am-3am. These backups are created once a day, late at night and are preserved indefinitely.

The other thing to keep in mind with FileMaker Cloud involves a restoration from a crash. If something goes wrong with FileMaker Cloud, there is no live person to call and talk to at FMI. You have to send an email to them, and they will respond to it during normal 8am-5pm PST business hours Monday through Friday.

The FileMaker Cloud technology is pretty reliable, but when it goes bad, people like to talk to a live person. Some of the senior staff at RCC have been burned by this, and refuse to use FileMaker Cloud for this specific reason. Other staff at RCC have not had any problems and tend to recommend FileMaker Cloud to their customers as an acceptable answer.

I think using FileMaker Cloud depends on two things:

      A) Limited budget to pay for dedicated IT staff

        and

      B) Your sensitivity to having a system down with no live people to talk to.

Database Backup Strategy - FileMaker Server (FMS)

FileMaker Server is often referred to as "on-premise server." The "on-premise" is a little misleading, but FileMaker Server would be the software you use if you host the database in your building. Also, you can install FMS on a Windows virtual server up in the cloud.

I am not going to give you explicit instructions on how to run your backups. I think your backup strategy will depend upon the size of your dataset and the budget of your customer.

I have a general rule that I do not want to lose more than 15 minutes of work.

My personal preference for RCC servers is we have separate scheduled backups that run every 15 minutes around the clock. These backups fire at 15-after, 30-after, and 45-after. We only retain two sequential copies of these backups.

For hourly backups (which run at the top of the hour), we retain at least 24 of these, sequentially. We write these to multiple drives. The 15-minute backups are written to a different drive.

There are also progressive backups, which only keep the last two copies. These are fairly automatic. I typically write these to a third drive. FMI, in their documentation, explicitly recommends that you do not write the progressive backups to the boot drive.

I also understand that there can be an earthquake, fire, or hurricane that can destroy the FileMaker server. So offsite backups are critical.

The trick is to make sure that you have good offsite backups. Amazon S3 can be loosely described as a giant Dropbox server up in the cloud that Amazon manages for you. Amazon does not like to use the word "Dropbox" because it is really not Dropbox.

From a business perspective, it is a giant file dumping ground where you can dump files into a directory that you control with your Amazon account. You can also do offsite backups to Dropbox or another service like that. Ideally, you would do offsite backups hourly. However, if the data set gets very large (more than 2-3 gigs) and the server is in your office, then doing hourly backups will probably strain your network connection. No Bueno!

> **TERMINOLOGY**
>
> FMI's Marketing team uses the term "progressive backups." FMI's Engineering team uses the term "incremental backups." I tend to get them confused, but both are accurate terms that describe that backup process.

> **TERMINOLOGY**
>
> "Amazon S3" is a web service offered by Amazon Web Services. Amazon S3 provides storage through web services interfaces.

> **TERMINOLOGY**
>
> "RAID (Redundant Array of Independent Disks)" is a data storage virtualization technology that combines multiple physical disk drive components into one or more logical units for the purposes of data redundancy, performance improvement, or both.

In a worse case scenario, you are going to write the backups offsite daily, in the middle of the night when things are quiet in the office. As a side note, some people like to run everything on RAID. I have never seen a RAID system, managed by local IT staff, operate properly during an emergency. I have very low confidence in your typical IT person being able to manage and restore a RAID system that has failed. A RAID system does not replace scheduled backups.

The idea with RAID is that you have four or five drives running. If one of them dies, then the remaining functional drives keep things running. This part of RAID systems tends to run successfully. However, trying to drop a new drive in and have the system rebuild itself has failed everytime I have seen it done. I am sure that giant corporate IT departments have dedicated staff who spend their entire days learning the ins and outs of these systems. However, at a basic power user level, or even a senior engineer level, this does not seem to work out well. So, I think there is limited application for RAID.

All drives should be using solid-state drives and not spinning drives. A couple of cloud-service providers still (in 2018) use spinning drives only. This can cause slow-downs in your FileMaker access.

In summary, FMI has no official recommendation on backup schedules. They do not want to be on the legal hook for any decisions you make. I think this is a legal issue and not so much a best practices issue.

My recommendation would be for you to consider all of the bad things that are likely to happen where you live. Fire? Hurricane? Earthquake? You need to make sure you can always get a fresh backup database and not have to use a crashed file.

Check Your Backups

Part of running a FileMaker server is setting it up and getting it running. The other part is performing a weekly database backup inspection. Some senior consultants are oblivious to this need. For a wide variety of reasons, it is possible for FileMaker Server to have the backup processes fail and you not be notified.

As a general rule, customers will never think to administer their FileMaker Cloud server. The other day I had a customer tell me, "Well, the server is running on Amazon and Amazon always takes care of the backups, so we never have to worry about it."

Nothing could be further from the truth. It is a good idea to check on the backups. The only thing Amazon does is provide reliable electrical power and internet connectivity to a virtual server.

FileMaker Server does have a notification system to email you if something goes wrong. However, the emails can fail. The emails could be marked "spam," or any other myriad of problems can occur. The short version is, do not trust FileMaker Server to tell you that it is not making backups. You need to visually inspect it each week to make sure that the backups are being written. This means investigating the offsite backup location, looking for the files, etc.

If you do not want to do this yourself, then you will need to have the customer sign-off and take over this responsibility on their end.

Types of Corruption

Structural & User Data Corruption: Typically, corruption will be in either the structure of the FileMaker file or the user input data. Going forward, I will call this "Structural Corruption" or "data Corruption." This sort of corruption is what we are always trying to avoid, and is bad. (See Next Sections)

Index Corruption: The index is what is used to drive relationships and the FIND command. Index corruption is NOT uncommon and is not really dangerous. FMI expects this will happen and has built features to specifically address this. The "index" is NOT the core data that users input.

Detecting Index corruption is pretty straightforward. A relationship will not work when it should, or a FIND command will obviously not find specific records that you "know" already exist.

To fix Index Corruption, you can dump the indexes.

Note: the user input data will not be harmed by dumping the indexes. FileMaker Pro will rebuild new indexes as it needs them. One method of rebuilding the indexes is to run the Recover command and specify the option to have FileMaker rebuild the indexes for you. It is an explicit checkbox. Alternatively, you can go into Field Definitions and turn OFF indexing for a field. FileMaker will re-create the indexes as needed.

YODA SAYS

Died many Bothan spies did, to bring us this information.

Structural Defects: This is something that is only known to FileMaker Engineers. In some previous versions of the FileMaker platform, certain bugs existed in FileMaker Pro or FileMaker Server. These resulted in something that most developers would describe as corruption, but it is not.

WTF? Yah, do not freak out. For example, in a version of FileMaker Server (around the FM8 days), when a user deleted a graphic off of a layout, the data was not deleted properly. It appeared to be deleted, but the graphic still lived inside of the FileMaker .fp7 file. FMI engineers

> **NOTE FROM RICHARD**
>
> While writing the update to this book, we actually ran into a new FileMaker 15 file that actually had a structural defect. The file was acting a little funky and after digging into it, we found the recovered library. At the time, the file was running "live" on a FileMaker Server. After quitting FileMaker Server and having it complete the shutdown process, the recovered library disappeared. So it is possible to have structural defects appear in modern versions of FileMaker. It may appear or disappear for reasons only known to FileMaker Inc.

found the bug and fixed it. However, because of the nature of the bug, they were unable to remove the graphic. It remains a buried artifact that lives inside of the file. Is the file corrupted? No. Is this weird? Yep!

The reason that I mention this is that someday you will probably see a new table added to your FileMaker file, called "Recovered Library." When you see this, the records in this table will include the remnants of this structural defect. Deleting the records and the table will remove this from your view. However, if you run the Recover command again, this table (and these records) will magically reappear. Does this cause problems in the database? No. So just ignore it.

Detecting Corruption (Structural and Data)

The way corruption is detected is when a user is using the file, and somewhere FileMaker Pro (or Go) crashes. It could be a bug in the product. That can happen on any release. So what do you look for? How can you tell something is corrupted?

Structural Corruption

Something I have seen periodically over the years is Structural Corruption. Typically, the user crashes FileMaker Pro when they visit, or print a specific layout. Ask yourself, "Can this behavior be repeated?". Well, if you just ran a Windows update, and now FileMaker Pro crashes, then this may be a Windows update issue.

Test the problem on other people's computers. If you are on Windows, test it on a Mac. Collect as much data as possible. If it seems like this is a problem with the database file, and not the FileMaker Pro App itself, then there is probably a corrupt object on the layout. This could be a field, a piece of text, a button, a graphic, etc. Any of these objects "could be damaged" and cause FileMaker to crash.

How do you fix it? Well, you need to find the bad object. Assuming that you can visually inspect the layout without crashing, the corrupted object will not be obvious. Duplicate the layout and remove half of the objects. Then retest. If the problem goes away, then one of the objects that you removed is the culprit. Now keep adding and removing the objects until you find the bad object.

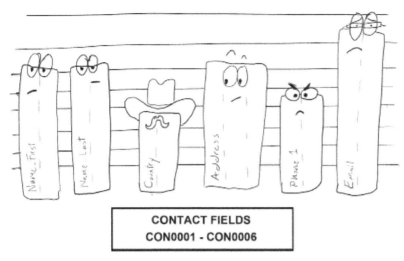

> **FYI**
> Corrupted objects will not identify themselves as being corrupt. A corrupted object tries to blend in with all of the normal good objects. Picking it out from a lineup will be difficult to impossible.

Once you have found the bad object, remove it from the layout. Yes, I said remove it. Do NOT copy it first. Nuke it! Then recreate it, from scratch. You can copy and paste the corruption back into the layout. No Bueno! Always create the replacement object from scratch!

As a side note: it is possible for a script, or a field definition, or even a TO, to get corrupted. The same rule applies. Either replace the entire file with a clean backup or manually remove the affected item and rebuild it.

Data Corruption

Keep in mind that your corruption may be in the user-entered data, and not in the file structure. For example, maybe the text in the description field is corrupted. If you are trying to reproduce the crash, does the crash seem specific to a specific record? Or, is the crash relative to a specific layout, regardless of the record?

If you determine that the data is corrupted, then you can clean it by one of two ways:

(A) Delete the record entirely, and then rekey it back in

OR

(B) Make a "Clone" of the FileMaker file. Then do a Tab-delimited export of the data. Close the damaged file. Open the Clone, and import it in the Tab-delimited file. Making a Tab or comma-delimited file will export ONLY the data, and any corruption is stripped out. Do not forget to reset any auto-generated primary keys.

Final Notes about Corruption

If you follow our guidelines about never using crashed files, then the previous section can be pretty much ignored, as you will never need to deal with it. But, if you are working on someone else's file, and you do not know the history, then be on the lookout.

Also, modern versions of FileMaker have a rugged Recover command. This command generates a log file which can be super useful for chasing down a bad object in FileMaker. A lot of people do not trust the Recover command and do not like to use the file it creates. That is a whole separate conversation. However, the Recover command does give you a couple pieces' of good info.

> (1) The Recover command generates a text log of everything that it finds. If it finds a bad object, it will tell you. The log is a bit cryptic. If you see an error message in the log, it applies to the item listed in the log that is directly above it (or the previous line).
>
> (2) At the end of the log, FileMaker Pro will pass official judgment on the file. Essentially, FMP will generate a "no errors found" or "errors found" message.

If you see the "no errors found" message; then the file is probably good. If you see the "errors found" message, then the file MIGHT be broken, or it may be just fine. That is the problem with the whole corruption/recovery conversation. There are perfectly functional files that have a single object that is broken, and that will result in the Error message. Can you keep using the file? Probably. Will it eventually quit working? Probably not.

I personally hate the vagueness of this. For that reason, I try to do everything to avoid this.

Whether you use the newly created recovery file is up to you. A lot of developers hate to do this. I would use it if that was the ONLY file I had left, and I did not have a clean backup.

That being said, the Recover command is super useful as it gives you a good indicator to the overall health of the FMP12 file. Is it perfect? No. But, it can tell you three basic things:

(1) Does FileMaker Pro see any errors?

(2) If Errors are spotted, it will tell you what the affected objects are.

(3) The end summary will give you an indication of the level of damage, if any. If you see one or two errors, then you can probably manually fix these. If the damage report looks extensive, then that tells you that you DEFINITELY need to use a different file.

8 Tools

Bug & To-Do Tracking

There is specialized software available for this sort of thing, but at the beginning a simple word processing document will suffice.

Create a document in your favorite word processor, title it MyProject_Bugs (or similar) and keep it open along side your project, whenever you are working. Store it in the documentation folder for your project. As you find bugs, or things that need to be done, or think of features you would like to add, enter them in detail into this document. Don't be lazy about this. It's important.

You will use this document extensively, and should refer to it daily. Don't delete items from it when they are done. Check them off, or move them to a different section of the document, but keep every entry. And when an entry is completed, note in detail what you did to fix the problem or add the feature, what build you did it in and the date.

For every new entry, religiously add the date the entry was made, and the build number to which the item refers. Also, be certain to note in which build a problem was found, fixed, or feature added. This is very important.

More than this, keep careful track of everything you do or change for every build. You might even want a separate word processor document for this. Or you may want to go so far as to copy and paste before and after calculation changes into such a document so you can refer to them later.

This way, when a new problem appears that was not in previous builds, you can track its origin through your notes and potentially solve it much more quickly. You'd be amazed just how easy it is to forget what you did yesterday that might have caused the new problem you are experiencing today.

There are existing online solutions, like Basecamp, which allow you to track and add bugs and issues that might exist in a FileMaker file. An online solution enables customers to access and see what your To-Do List is, which helps improve your communication with them. If they can see your To-Do List, it helps reinforce your current status, as far as where you are at with the project. RCC will sometimes use our internal Issue Tracking database, without paying for Basecamp. We already bought FileMaker, and we love it. So why not use it? Basecamp is pretty advanced; you do not have to build anything, you just have to be willing to pay the monthly fee for the privilege of using the software.

Building on a FileMaker server

Another semi-controversial idea is using a FileMaker Server for your development process. Because of the inherent reliability of the modern FileMaker platform, a lot of teams, including my own, will tend to host a FileMaker solution on a FileMaker Server (or FileMaker Cloud) and develop against that "live" file. There are many critical benefits to doing this.

As stated previously, we have this unbreakable rule to "never use a crashed FileMaker file." If you are running a FileMaker file locally while doing development and you somehow manage to crash FileMaker, you need to throw that file away. Switch to the last good backup! It does not matter if you have spent a day, week or a year of work on it, that file should be tossed out.

If you are running local FileMaker files, you should think about closing and backing up the file every hour or two, then open up a copy and continue to work. A developer who is working on a local file, who then crashes the file, will have an incentive to continue to use the crashed file. This is very bad.

So, to remove the temptation, and prevent this problem, the file needs to run on a FileMaker Server. It is very rare that a FileMaker client will crash a FileMaker Server.

If a FileMaker client is working on a file hosted by FileMaker Server and it crashes, the server "gracefully" disconnects the user. This "graceful" disconnect works to protect the FileMaker file so it can continue to run on the server without affecting other users. So, crashing FileMaker Pro, while accessing a remotely connected file, is no big deal.

Twenty years ago, this crash was a problem with the FileMaker platform. Back then, crashing Pro could wipe out your file, even though it was running on Server. With modern versions of FileMaker, FMI has spent a lot of time implementing protections to keep a FileMaker file from being damaged.

Build a Tips & Techniques Database

You will get lots of tips and techniques from mailing lists and websites. You will lose track of most of them. When you need to use a technique you've used before, you either have to hunt for it all over again, or pull it out of a project you've used it on.

Build a simple database to keep track of all these things. It will save you a lot of time hunting. You'd be surprised how many times you can use a technique and still not remember how it was done the next time you need it. RCC maintains a random "junk drawer database" for this kind of stuff, which we call the Dead Bird database.

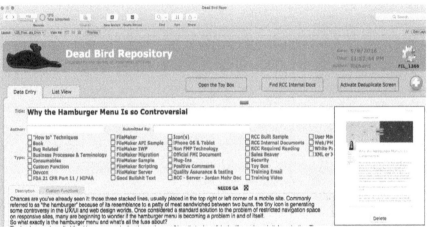

One of my rescue cats tends to bring me live rattlesnakes that it has captured. This can be stressful.

The "dead bird" idea. If you know anything about cats, they like to bring dead animals to you to show you their love and value to the team. If you are a manager of a FileMaker consultancy, then you will have FileMaker developers that do the same thing.

Some of our FileMaker developers tend to build various tricks, or one-off techniques, or find something on the internet and bring it to our team in the same way that a cat brings you a dead bird. Instead of losing track of all of these random little nuggets of knowledge, we save them in the Dead Bird database.

Create a Developer's Template

A lot of developers recommend maintaining a library of pre-canned features and solutions that you can recycle. However, a vast majority of these are low quality. If you don't have a recyclable set of awesome features, then my recommendation would be to start with a copy of FM Starting Point as a repository for your cool features you want to save. FM Starting Point is the most popular free starter solution worldwide.

The design is maintained by Nicolas Hunter, who previously worked for FileMaker Inc. as part of their design team.

> **FYI**
>
> Nick also makes a number of user interface files that are designed to a very high UI/UX standard. Feel free to check out other available samples at
>
> http://bit.ly/FMSPmarket17

Buy a Computer

No, I don't get any kickbacks from computer manufacturers. But you still need a new computer if you currently have only one.

If you work on a Mac, buy a Windows machine (oh, stop groaning). If you work on a Windows machine, buy a Mac (you too, quit it!). To make things even more exciting for your credit card, you probably need an iPhone, iPad and potentially even an Android device, if your customers are actively using that platform.

FileMaker is a *cross-platform* database and that is the way it is deployed. If you don't have a cross-platform development environment, then expect your customers to point out your sloppy design practices as they visually test your software. It is just a matter of whether you want to look stupid or not.

In an ideal world, you need to see what your databases look like in all of the environments that your customer plans to use. Before you build 200 layouts that look good on one platform, you need to make sure those layouts look good on the platforms that are likely to access them. Once again, this goes back to talking to your customer about how they are going to use the solution before you build it.

Don't believe your client when he tells you they have only one type of machine and will never have the other. Chances are they will. And even if they do not, you may one day want to adapt this solution for another client who has the other platform.

When your customer tells you they only use one type of computer or platform, make sure you confirm that conversation in an email. That way you have a legal paper conversation to fall back on when they change their mind.

Also, there are minor differences in the behavior of some FileMaker functions such as popup menus, between Mac and Windows versions, as well as FileMaker Go and WebDirect. You need to be certain that what you build works on both platforms. (Example: the Insert from Device script step works differently between Desktop, iOS, and WebDirect.)

9 Techniques

The Correct Relational Graph

One of the hardest things new FileMaker developers try to understand is the idea of how they should organize the relational graph in FileMaker. After the release of FileMaker 7, one of the more enterprising contributors to the FileMaker community developed the idea of the anchor/buoy method for organizing the relational graph.

The anchor/buoy method is a process that you follow with specific rules that help to keep things simple. More importantly, it allows people who come after you to easily understand what you were doing as you built your FileMaker solution.

DOWNLOAD

Download the Anchor Buoy extract here:

http://bit.ly/FMAnchorBuoyExcerpt17

At one point FileMaker Incorporated semi-formally endorsed the use of anchor/buoy to a degree where it was an official part of their curriculum/textbook. Currently, FMI makes no recommendations on the organization of the relational graph.

Because I train thousands of people in the FileMaker platform (yes, no joke it is thousands) the anchor/buoy is one of the most important lessons to teach them.

After talking with some of the gnomes at FileMaker, I found out why FileMaker decided to remove the endorsement of the anchor/buoy. They had a belief that use of the anchor/buoy would result in slow performance of your FileMaker solution.

FYI

FileMaker Konferenz, Salzburg - 10/2017 HOnza Koudelka "Latest FMP/FMS Performance Questions & Test Results". This link may change:

http://bit.ly/DevCon_Honza17

However, in 2017, Honza Koudelka, from 24U, gave a presentation at DevCon Europe on the performance speeds and differences between using a spider graph and using an anchor/buoy graph. Honza found, despite claims to the contrary, the anchor/buoy graph was either as fast as or faster than the other methodologies. So, "slow performance" is not a reason to dump anchor/buoy.

We cover understanding anchor/buoy a great deal more in our FileMaker Pro video training course. The short version of the idea is that layouts are **only** attached to "Anchors" (TOs on the left side). All of the items that are necessary to support that layout, through a relationship, become child relationships (TOs on the right side), which are the "Buoys."

See the screenshot example below:

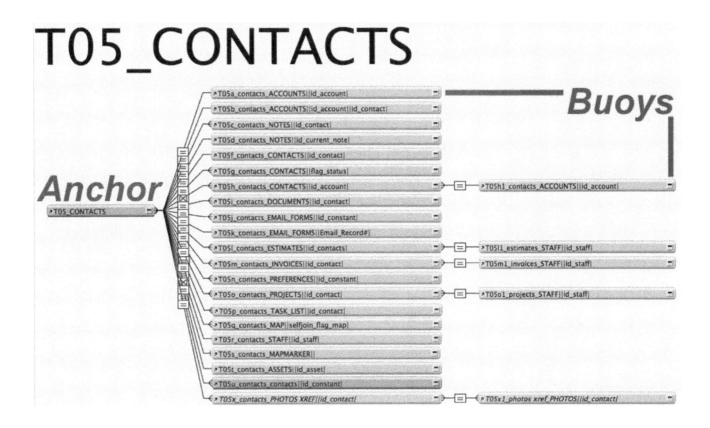

Every once in awhile someone will come to me, claiming one methodology has some abstract benefit, this is not uncommon. However, if you are senior enough to understand and argue the benefits of one methodology over the other, then you probably should not be reading this book. This book is intended for beginning and intermediate developers, not senior developers with fifteen years of development experience.

VIDEO TIP - 17 PLATFORM VIDEO COURSE

To learn more about Anchor/Buoy, watch videos "1130 - Anchor Buoy Design Methodology Part 1" and "1131 - Anchor Buoy Design Methodology Part 2".

Check Your Buttons

Previously I mentioned that buttons that have no action should not be shown on a layout unless they are grayed-out, making it clear to the user that they are non-functional under the current circumstances.

There used to be all sorts of tricks to accomplish this, but these days it is simple. At the most basic level, you can take a FileMaker button object, right-click it and change the conditional formatting of the button. Conditional formatting allows us to specify colors of the text, fill color, etc. of an object. Change the fill color of the button to grey to indicate the button is not currently available.

The second half of making a button that does not function is to adjust the script that the button runs. Make sure to include a calculation that prevents the button from running, if the button is greyed out. Whatever calculation we use in the conditional formatting; we also use in an "If" statement at the beginning of the script that the button runs. So, if a user is inclined to press a greyed out button, nothing will happen.

Technical Debt

Invariably there is going to be some "technical debt" in a FileMaker custom application. Technical debt is a new term for an old concept.

Technical debt means there is some design, code, or usage limitation of the software. The technical debt is similar to running up debt on a credit card. The longer you live with the technical debt, the more painful it will be to dig your way out of that problem to fix it.

For example, we have talked previously about how a customer misuses a Contact database that runs in FileMaker. Every time the customer has a meeting, they copy and paste the notes into the first field they see on the Contacts layout. The customer does not have an appropriate notes field; this is technical debt.

The more that users misuse the database, putting data into incorrect locations, the more debt they are accruing. Eventually, the technical debt will cause substantial problems. This results in wasted time and effort of the staff, that could be used for profitable activities. Let us dive into this.

Impossible Data

Previously I've discussed the fact that you will sometimes be called upon to build a new database to replace an unsalvageable existing solution. Unfortunately, this does not mean you won't have to deal with the old database. In fact, you'll probably have to deal with it quite a lot. The reason is simple: it's full of data! Data you have to move into or otherwise account for in your new solution.

The worse the design of the original solution, the more trouble you will have moving the data it contains. To the novice this probably sounds odd. After all, FileMaker has both export and import functions that work quite well. What's the problem?

The problem is that poorly designed databases invariably have data stored in a table where it should not be and also have lots and LOTS of data stored in inappropriate fields. Data is stored in inappropriate fields because users had no place else to put it.

One of the most common occurrences is finding a single table containing data that should have been placed in multiple tables.

Imagine a single table containing what should have been two, three, four or more tables, with hundreds of bits and pieces of data in the wrong fields. This is a problem you certainly will not solve with a simple export and import. What can you do? That's what this topic is about: dealing with impossible data.

The following examples reference tools, some of which are available only in newer versions of FMP. You can do all of these things in other versions, it's just a little more tedious. The important thing here is to get the big idea; all else follows.

Let's imagine you have a single table with contacts and multiple addresses for those contacts stored in the same table (trust me, it will never be this simple). Some of the contacts have one address, others three or four. You have to do a lot of sorting and reporting based on addresses, so leaving them where they are is not an option. They must be split out into a separate table.

To start, you must think of this single table as two separate tables that are stuck together. The address fields are part of a distinct table that just happens to have the wrong primary key and no foreign key at all, associated with each address record.

So... put a foreign key in!

Add a stored calculation field that is equal to the existing primary key for the table. Often, there will not be a proper primary key. So create and populate a primary key field first.

Once you leave the define fields dialog box, the new foreign key calculation field will automatically fill itself with the matching primary key. Go right back into the field definition area and convert the same foreign key calculation field to a simple number field. It will retain the numbers just entered into it via the calculation. You now have your foreign key.

Duplicate the table and create a relationship between the primary key in the old table and the newly created foreign key in the new table. The new table will still have the old primary key field in it. Change its name to reflect the new table and reset it to start entering numbers at one (1). This will be your primary key for the new table. (Remember, the old table did not have a primary key for the address records.)

Delete all the records from this duplicated table. Now you should have an empty, duplicated table, the primary key of which has been suitably renamed and reset to start numbering records at one. Delete all the data fields that don't apply to this new *addresses* table.

If you have four sets of address fields in the old table, you will have to do four imports into the new table, one for each address set. Remember to first go to the proper layout for the original table and select Show All Records from the records menu first (any records not in the current found set will not be available to the import command). Then go to a layout for your new table, select the import records command and in the import records dialog box, set the import list to matching field names. Deselect all fields except the newly created foreign key field and the first set of address fields. Be sure to check Perform auto-enter options while importing so that the primary key field of the new table will be populated. The newly imported records will already contain the proper foreign key entries because you created them in the old table before importing.

Just repeat the above import process for each succeeding set of address fields, and you'll have your new address table fully populated and properly related to the contacts table. Remember to change the fields selected for import with each successive selection. (Repeat the whole process for any other data sets you need to break out of the old table into new ones.) Throw a portal into the mix and pat yourself on the back when you notice it's not empty. Now just delete all those address fields from the old table. You don't need them there any more.

Breaking data out of one table and into multiple tables isn't too difficult; it's just tedious. In the case of data contained in the wrong fields, the problem is a bit more gritty.

You'll find phone numbers tacked onto the end of name and address fields or in note fields. You may find two phone numbers in one phone number field, two email addresses in one email address field. The variations are endless and you have to clean it up because the data is useless as is. Unless there are very few records indeed, you simply can't clean it all up by hand, it would take forever. Automation is the only answer. To deal with the mess you'll have to resort to thinking outside the box quite a bit. The approach you take will depend a great deal on the manner in which data is messed up in the field(s). But, I'll give you a general idea to get you started...

Let's assume you are dealing with a name field, and that many of the records also contain phone numbers, email addresses and the name of a second person all in that same name field. (Don't dwell too heavily on the particular types of data I've chosen for this example. It is the overall concept you must grasp, rather than the specific data types.)

Return to the calculation field trick mentioned above. Create a stored calc field that equals the content of the offending field, but uses the Trim() function to make sure you don't have any superfluous spaces at the beginning or end of the new field. I also use a triple-nested

Substitute() function that replaces two spaces with one. This way multiple spaces are replaced with one space only. Include other functions that may help clean up the data initially as dictated by what you find. Leave the define fields dialog in order to cause the field to populate (assume this from now on, so I don't have to keep repeating it). Then return to define fields and convert this new calc field to a text field. The following is very important!

The new field you just created is now your working field. Don't touch the field definition or alter the data in this or the original field for any reason. You are going to alter data from the working field with calculations in additional new fields and *you will make mistakes*!

You must have an untouched field with the original data intact and an untouched working field with the original data minus superfluous spaces, so that you can start over if one of your calcs blows up in your face. As you progress, be sure to copy and paste the various calcs you create into a word processor document so that you can quickly paste them back into FMP and use them again if you need to start over.

The next step is to create additional calc fields that manipulate the data from your new working field. For each possible type of misplaced data you will create a new set of calc fields. These calc fields will occur in hierarchies. One hierarchy for each piece of data you wish to break out. Remember that you don't want to lose all those email addresses, phone numbers and extra names, so this effort is going to get complicated.

You will need a set of calc fields that removes email addresses, phone numbers and extra names, leaving single names. (You will need another set of fields that removes names and phone numbers, leaving email addresses, and still another that removes names and email addresses, leaving only phone numbers. But we'll skip these for ease of illustration purposes.) The example here is further simplified by ignoring the fact that we may have name fields with two or more email addresses and/or two or more phone numbers in them, in addition to one or two names.

Here are some hints that will help you to understand the kind of logic needed with this sort of data cleanup problem:

- *All email addresses contain the @ symbol, so we can easily identify any name field that contains an email address (Duh! OK, so this one's obvious).*
- *No name in any language of which I am aware contains any digits. However, an email address can contain digits. Therefore, a field that contains no @ symbol, but does contain digits, must contain a phone number (unless the field contains the person's shoe size… but let's not complicate this). This means that in fields that might contain an email address and a phone number, the email address must be stripped out first.*
- *Names present a little tougher challenge. If everyone's name consisted of*

just a first and last name, it would be simple. A field cleaned of email addresses and phone numbers would have two words in it if it contained a single name and four words if it contained two names. Unfortunately life doesn't work that way. You could have names like: John Public, John Q. Public, J.Q. Public, J. Public, John Public Sr., John Quincy Public Jr., etc. The possible variations are daunting, preventing you from taking a simple approach like LeftWords (nameField, 2). However, the problem is not unsolvable.

Any field with only two words in it is a field containing a single person's name. The same is still somewhat true of a three-word field; no one is likely to enter just a first or last name for a second person. The first point of suspicion is when a field contains four words or more. That could be a two-name field, but it could also contain John Q. Public Sr. or John Quincy Public MD. (Keep that cyanide capsule handy if the field contains Dr. & Mrs. John Quincy Abraham Public III.)

Search the database for name fields (cleaned of phones and email addresses) longer than three words to look for patterns then take advantage of those patterns in your subsequent calc fields. I won't go into detail here. That would require its own book, but you get the idea... A four-word field where the second word has a length of one means the second word is an initial and therefore the field can't contain two names. A four-word field that contains MD, M.D., Sr., Jr. etc., can't contain two names either. Grin and bear it. The logic will come to you and you'll be able to whittle the problem down to only a few fields that must be fixed by hand.

Note: The foregoing by the way, is an excellent reason you must not build a solution that allows users to put an entire name in one field, but instead should always break the name up into first, middle, and last name fields. A single field for a name is an invitation to throw junk data into the field. It is somewhat less likely to occur to users to put an email address or an additional person's name into a first or last name only field.

- *For fields containing two person's names, you do not have to get both names out, just the first. The second name is a snap (see next bullet point).*
- *Once you have achieved a clean name field, retrieving the phone number, email address or a second person's name from the original working field is much simpler. Using the Substitute () function, a new calc field can remove the clean names, clean email addresses or clean phone numbers from data it pulls from the working field, leaving only the required data. Just play with it, you'll get it. The trick is the Substitute () function and a healthy sprinkling of Trim () functions.*
- *Run tests on the data you are trying to control, using custom dialogs to discover if FMP is seeing the data the same way you are. For example,*

the @ symbol will tell you an email address exists, but it won't tell you where it starts and ends. The email address fredmertz@aol.com is seen by FMP as two words: fredmertz and aol.com. (That's right, the dot is not seen as a word separator while the @ symbol is.) But fred_mertz@ aol.com is seen as three words: fred, mertz, and aol.com. FMP sees the underscore character between fred and mertz as a word separator. So, using words to determine the position of an email address won't work. However, spaces will!

There are no spaces in email addresses, so the first space to the left of the @ symbol shows you the beginning of the email address, while the first space to its right shows you the end. However, an email address might be contained between parentheses, brackets, quotes, etc. instead of spaces. So you may have to replace these with spaces. (Always step back and take a broader view.)

Below you will find a pair of diagrams illustrating the process. Be forewarned. These are over-simplified, particularly with reference to splitting up multiple names. Splitting disparate data out of single fields can be a genuine nightmare (and brain bender), but it is infinitely better than trying to do the job manually over thousands of records. One tool that is quite helpful is to create a temporary list layout that shows your successive calc fields side-by-side. This makes it easier to see what is working and what is not.

The circles with grayed-out text in the first illustration represent the working fields for salvaging telephone and email data (not covered further in the illustration). The octagon fields represent the calc fields used to process the names contained in the original data fields.

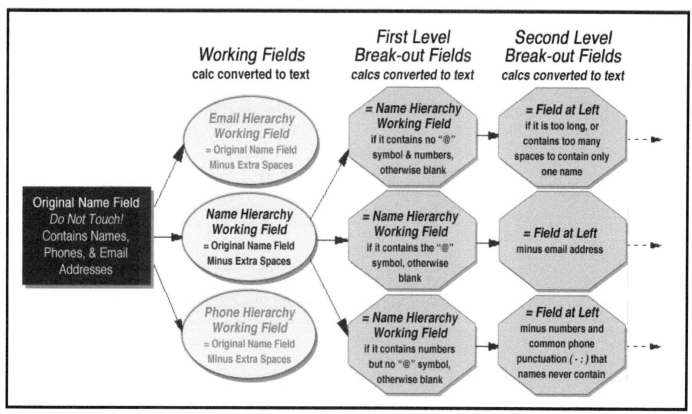

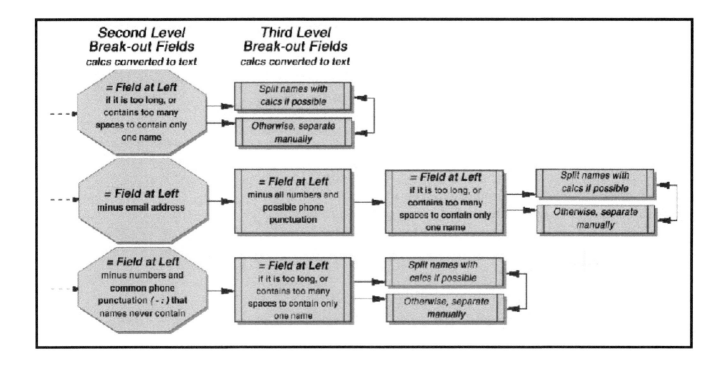

The octagon fields in the second illustration are the same as the right hand set of fields in the first. They are there for visual continuity and to indicate that the second illustration is a continuation of the first.

The approach described here involves cleaning up names first, leaving phone numbers and email addresses for later. This is not the only approach and not necessarily even the best. You could start by cleaning up email addresses (you can't start with phone numbers because, as mentioned previously, an email address can contain numbers) then phone numbers, saving names for last. In fact, this could be easier. Each case is different, and you will absolutely have to experiment and fail a few times before you find the best approach to cleaning messy data. Messy data is like the messes kids make: each mess is different and more creative than the last!

Alternate Methods of Dealing with Technical Debt

As you can see from the previous conversation, the correction of database issues and the resulting bad data can be expensive, if it is even doable. As an alternate suggestion, instead of trying to concoct ways of cleaning random technical debt, it may be beneficial for the customer to hire a temporary employee. The temp staff, can copy and paste the data from the old system and correctly paste or load it into the new system.

This may seem like a goofy way to solve the problem. However, using a temp to "brute force the fix" may be far more cost-effective and painless for everyone involved. Four weeks of temporary time, at a pay rate of $15/hour will be more cost-effective, and frankly less risky, than a week of serious coding.

Keep in mind, that if you decide to program your way out of technical debt, you need to have the skills to pull it off. Sometimes it is not worth the stress, especially if you are not the person responsible for the creation of the technical debt. So, consider the brute force method as a potential answer to the resolution of technical debt.

10 Gotchas

Mixing Versions of FileMaker

> **TERMINOLOGY**
> Reminder, we use "FMI" to indicate the company - FileMaker Inc. - not the platform.

In recent years FMI has begun shipping major releases every twelve months, typically in May. FMI has never formally committed to this, and it is not on their website.

However, if you listen to their executives talk in public settings, you will frequently hear this messaging. Because the updates are more frequent, you are more likely to see a customer deployment that spans across more than one version of the FileMaker platform.

For example, if FileMaker 17 is shipping you may have customers that are using Go 16, Pro 16 and/or Pro 15, and maybe a Server that is a different version altogether.

> **FYI**
> Pro 17 and Go 17 can't talk to a 14 Server.

The problem is, without first checking the FileMaker website, you are never quite sure which versions of FileMaker you can mix together. It would be great if FMI came up with a formal policy on this. In meetings, I have personally encouraged them to come up with a standard version mixing policy.

However, every time they release a product, the approved list of compatible versions is different. In short, there is zero consistency regarding what versions FMI is going to allow you to mix from one release to the next.

FMI seems to be a little more consistent regarding the versions they allow you to use with FileMaker Cloud. You must use matching versions of the client and the cloud. Otherwise, the clients will not be able to connect. If you are using FileMaker Cloud 16, you can use FileMaker Pro 16 or FileMaker 17. If you are using FileMaker Cloud 17, you can only use the FileMaker 17 clients. With FileMaker Server 17, you can use Pro and Go 15, 16, and 17 clients and you can expect these to change without rhyme or reason within the next release.

> **TERMINOLOGY**
> "QA" stands for Quality Assurance testing. QA testing burns a huge chunk of FMI's annual budget. So it is not a trivial effort.

In all fairness to FMI, the company has to balance security concerns and the cost of QAing on previous versions of the product to work with new releases, as well as overall profitability.

As an outside developer, I am never quite sure which specific concern is driving a particular list of compatible products. I think the underlying rules you need to understand are the following:

1) Do not try to anticipate what FMI is going to do in the next release.

2) Do not promise anything to the customer until you have printed out the compatibility sheet from the FileMaker website.

To find the compatibility of the products, go to their website, click the "Products" button and scroll to the bottom where the individual products are listed. Click on the product, then click the "Technical Specs" button on the top right of the screen.

Sending Email Out of FileMaker

The "Send Email" command in the FileMaker platform feels like the same command that we had from 1999. The Send Email command only sends out a plain text email (no HTML styling). It makes for the ugliest email that you could send to a customer. There is also a limitation of one attachment per email.

Oversights like this, continue to be one of the driving reasons why 360Works (out of Atlanta, GA) continues to be in business. RCC uses the 360Works Email plugin to generate HTML emails.

It seems every database RCC produces uses this plugin. Why, Because customers do not like plain text emails. I am personally thankful that 360Works builds and maintains a high-quality email plugin.

Shared Hosting

For decades, FileMaker development companies and hosting providers would set up FileMaker servers and rent out slices of that server. Businesses who needed a FileMaker solution hosted would pay a minimal monthly fee for this.

FMI officially terminated this as a legal option, starting with the release of FileMaker 15. To minimize the squealing and complaining from the FileMaker development community, FMI did not make this legal constraint retroactive. So, new releases of the product, starting with 15, do not legally permit shared hosting. Of course, people who were already using shared hosting with FileMaker Server 14, are allowed to continue.

Sometimes this is used as a justification not to upgrade and leads to customers trying to use newer clients with the 14 Servers.

Eventually, if you do not upgrade you are going to build technical debt and it will cost your business through functionality, compatibility, stability, or even security.

Starting with FileMaker 15, each company or organization is required to have their own FileMaker Server. The good news is that FileMaker Cloud is available which provides cost-effective hosting on a per-user basis. By using FileMaker Cloud, you can get an inexpensive virtual server running on Amazon's AWS data center.

> **VIDEO TIP - 17 PLATFORM VIDEO COURSE**
> To learn more about FileMaker Cloud, watch video "1601 - 90 Second Overview - FileMaker Cloud" and the whole "1600 - FileMaker Cloud" section.
>
> http://bit.ly/FMCloudOverview17

Runtimes

Since the advent of FileMaker 3, there has been the ability to create a "runtime solution" with the advanced version of Pro. A user who uses a runtime solution is not required to purchase a copy of FileMaker Pro. They just need the FileMaker file, and a runtime application, which is a stripped-down copy of FileMaker Pro. It would seem that using runtime is the perfect tool to build your vertical-market application.

Except, it is not.

When you create a commercial FileMaker application; the runtime is a limited copy of FileMaker Pro that is permanently attached to your commercial solution.

> **TERMINOLOGY**
> A "runtime" is a special stripped-down copy of FileMaker Pro that will only run a specific FileMaker solution. The runtime allows a user to use Browse Mode, Find Mode, and Preview Mode. There is no editing of scripts or database schema.

First, you build your FileMaker application using FileMaker Pro. Once this app is complete, you "give birth" to the runtime application using FileMaker Pro Advanced. Then, bundle your solution with the runtime and resell it to your customers. FMI won't get any royalties.

If you consider this a good idea, I will urge you to reconsider basic capitalism. Organizations and individuals who provide services for free (when other people around them are making money) tend to get agitated and pissed off.

As you may guess, FMI has not been financially incentivized to maintain or promote the runtime feature. In fact, several years ago, FMI officially announced that it would be depreciated and officially removed from the platform. As a result of this and other "gotcha" issues, there has been a lot of complaining and whining by some people in the FileMaker community.

Now, I consider it grossly disingenuous for people to get something for free and continue to demand the free thing is updated and continuously made available. This is a form of corporate welfare where Apple Computer and FMI are effectively subsidizing or providing a free product that you can utilize for the benefit of your personal business.

I do not have a lot of sympathy for these kinds of people. However, that does not stop the complaining and whining online when FMI indicated they would discontinue this feature.

The FileMaker runtime is going to go away. However, I am confident that if you were to write a cheque to FileMaker for a million dollars, they would probably reconsider their support for the runtime.

> **← IMPORTANT**
>
> Technically, FileMaker Pro Advanced is not free. A perpetual license of FileMaker Pro Advanced is about $540/year. FMI is not currently offering a single user annual license for Pro Advanced.

Getting Old and Grumpy

The FileMaker platform has been around for a long time. There are a large number of people who have been using FileMaker for decades, and they are getting to retirement age. Unfortunately, a number of these people prefer FileMaker the way it used to be fifteen years ago. As new forward-facing features come out, these people tend to complain that FileMaker has become too complicated.

Fortunately, FMI sees fit to continue to update the product and make it relevant in a modern world. I am personally terrified of the fact that I may become old and grumpy someday. I frequently remind myself to be objective and open to new ideas and new features within the FileMaker platform.

If you want to live a long and healthy life, my suggestions to you are to get out and try new things and try not to get too grumpy with FMI when your favorite features from twenty years ago change.

Web API Integration

An example of one new-fangled gadget FMI has added to the toolkit is the ability to connect to outside websites and services easily.

For example, I have personally been creating invoices in FileMaker since 1990. In the last year, it has become straight-forward to connect FileMaker to PayPal. This process allows you to create an invoice in FileMaker and send the invoice to PayPal. PayPal emails the customer and collects the payment, then communicates back to FileMaker that money was collected and deposited. This eliminates the hassles of directly processing credit cards and greatly simplifies the entire workflow.

> **TERMINOLOGY**
>
> This section deals with integrating outside services into the FileMaker platform. Specifically we are talking about using the insert URL scrpt step to talk to REST based services. In plain english, this is the consumption of data by FileMaker. This is different than using FileMaker as a data source which is often referred to as the "FileMaker Data API."

> **FYI**
>
> FM Starting Point Enhanced (FMSPe) is only available by purchasing the Complete Learning FileMaker Subscription Annual Software and Training Bundle:
>
> http://bit.ly/LFSubscribe17

My team actually built this functionality into FM Starting Point Enhanced, making it available to everyone. One of the developers for RCC specifically sat down to investigate communicating with PayPal. PayPal documents how to communicate with it, using a series of Open URL commands.

This modern communication method (using URLs) is called "REST" or "REST API." In our example, PayPal decided to support REST technology; then they were nice enough to provide documentation on how to connect to their service. You also hear this referred to as an "API connection." But we are not limited to PayPal. Almost every major service in the world has a REST API connection to it.

Technical Conversation:

> **FYI**
>
> This Web API conversation was partially written by one of RCC's senior engineers, Michael Wallace (see About the Author page).

The set of tools you will use to work with APIs are the "Insert From URL" script set, that has been beefed-up considerably in FMP16. There are also a series of FileMaker functions designed to work with JSON. JSON, or JavaScript Object Notation, is a data format that allows you to store complex, relational data in a flat text format. This is one of two primary formats in which APIs will answer you after you have "asked your question." The other one, which is less common nowadays, is XML. The FMP16 JSON functions make it easier for you to form the question in a way that an API is likely to understand and get the parts of the answer from the API in which you are interested.

There seem to be APIs for everything. This abundance of APIs has allowed users and companies to stand on the shoulders of giants with both information access and performing powerful tasks. A lot of major companies and services like Google, Amazon, Square, PayPal, etc. provide API access to their services and data. Upon doing a quick web search for "public API list," I found the first result provided a list of almost 500 APIs that are available for free, or a reasonable fee, which gives access to information and power far beyond that of mortal man.

So where to start? I would recommend getting familiar with the JSON data format and making web requests. There are free resources both in the general IT world and in the FileMaker universe that will help you work with different APIs. Postman has a free product to help you format the API "question" and test what "answers" you get back from your various requests. There are even tools that will create a large portion of FileMaker scripts and calculations for you once you tell them what the API expects.

FileMaker has come through with strong support for REST. This improvement, which came out with FileMaker 16, allows us to connect our silos of information to a much larger universe. Now you can leverage the services of others to accomplish tasks that were never before possible in FileMaker. Welcome to a brave new world!

NOTE FROM RICHARD
While connecting with an API seems like an advanced skillset, many of RCC's intermediate and junior engineers are learning the processes of connecting with REST API.

11 Miscellaneous

New Layouts

Newly created layouts always come with a couple of things you may not need: a header and a footer. If you are uncertain, delete them. You can always add them back in later. The exception to this is a printing layout. You'll probably need them here.

Headers in particular can get in your way if you don't really need them. Data you may wish to display near the top of your layout(s) may not display properly if contained in a header. Don't simply let FMP decide for you what you need in your layout. Put these layout parts in only if you need them.

Wait, What Changed?

You probably cannot tell the difference between an old version and the new version of your solution and your customers definitely cannot.

Previously, we discussed why your customers should never have access to old versions of a solution, because they can mistakenly open an old copy, thinking that they are in the new, hosted, live version and make data changes.

Then, the customer quits FileMaker, and comes back to work and will be shocked that their data is missing. Well, they put their new data in the old file, which is probably in the Trash Can. The same problem can occur to developers.

As you work on a solution, you will inevitably need to reopen a previous build (copy) of that solution to see what a field definition, script, layout setup or other item looked like previously. Or you may need to copy something from the old version into the newer. Whatever the purpose, this is a frequent occurrence and one of the many reasons to save builds often. It is also a great big bear trap.

When you go to examine something in that previous build, it is not uncommon to get engrossed in what you are doing and forget that you are in the *wrong file!* It may be only a few minutes, or it may take hours for you to realize that all your hard work has been wasted on an older and now useless version of your project. You will have to go back to the correct file and then backtrack as best you can to redo all the work you have just done. Naturally, you won't remember exactly what new code you entered into the incorrect file instead of the correct one.

Elsewhere in this book, I recommend buying a second development machine (Mac if you are on Windows and vice versa). Here is another excellent reason for that second machine. When you need to open an old build, do it on your other machine so that there is no chance you will erroneously start adding new code to a dead, archived copy.

Another Case for Multiple Machines

Previously, we discussed the need to have multiple computers on your desk, allowing you to keep your tasks and testing separate. Another critical area where this is super useful is for setting up security privileges in the FileMaker platform.

To set up the security for a FileMaker file, you first want to host the file on FileMaker Server or FileMaker Cloud. While we cover this in our video training course, in detail, it is worth noting here as well. Having multiple machines allows you to set the security privileges on one computer and then simultaneously test those changes on the second computer.

VIDEO TIP - 17 PLATFORM VIDEO COURSE
To learn more about test security privileges, watch video "1203 - Extended Privileges...the Basics".

Without the second machine, you are going to be constantly logging in and out of the system. This becomes a real drag, and you will not take the necessary time to do a good job testing. So you absolutely need to have at least two computers on your desk. As a general rule, I like to have at least two machines on my desk, one of which has two monitors. At my home office, in Fairfield, I actually have four machines, two of which each have double monitors. This allows me to test multiple versions at the same time, while also managing the company operations.

Limit the Time You Work on Your Solution

Don't work more than 35 hours on a solution in one week, or more than 7-8 hours in a day. We've all heard tales about programmers staying up all night with a case of Rockstar and a box of Twinkies. The truth is that programming is mentally exhausting work and as you reach the aforementioned limits, your productivity will drop precipitously. To continue working beyond these limits will be a waste of time and only force you to spend more time later, fixing what you fouled up when you were too tired to be working effectively.

I've lost count of how many times I've kept working on a problem until late at night, only to have the solution come to me in minutes the next morning. You gain nothing with long hours, except an early demise. There are quicker and more pleasant ways to do yourself in.

Another reason to not spend long hours working on a solution is that sitting at a desk for extended amounts of time is not good for your health. It can lead to gaining extra pounds as well joint and back issues. I would recommend setting up a powered standing desk so you can stand and work throughout the day. Another good practice is to schedule breaks throughout the day to go for a walk or to get on an exercise bike. This will provide a break for your body and mind.

I am experimenting with having my engineers sit on exercise bikes in the offices during our morning staff meetings. So from 9:15-10 am they would be on a conference call as well as be pedaling on an exercise bike. This solves two problems at once.

Now some developers swear that they are going to get a gym membership and do that in the evening. That almost never works out. It is better to just address it during the day by eating healthy, standing at your desk for at least part of the day, and moving around throughout the day.

I have several cats that are "festively plump." This is useful to slow them down so I can catch them and pet them. However, what may be marginally okay for a cat is definitely going to be unhealthy for you. While I love my kitties, I love you more. So please take care of yourself.

Building Commercial Software

Many, many newly-minted FileMaker developers get to a point with whatever it is they may be building when they say to themselves...

Hey, I could turn this into a product and sell it!

No you can't!

Wash your mouth out with soap and never allow that thought to traverse your frontal lobes again!

End of topic.

Oh, all right, if you're going to complain that much, I'll elaborate, but just a little. There are two types of vertical market software a FileMaker developer may consider building/selling:

- *a tool, plugin or module for other FMP developers to use in their solutions*
- *a software package to sell to a specific profession or industry aka, a "vertical market application."*

Building a vertical market application is something that is appealing to entrepreneurs. It is the "calling" and the draw of making an awesome product, and also making some money that inspires them. However, this is fraught with a great many dangers.

This is such a big topic in the FileMaker community that I made a dedicated video course on it, called "FileMaker for Startups and Entrepreneurs." This course is relatively inexpensive and I highly, highly recommend you watch it. My goal is not to talk you in or out of building a vertical market application, but it is to educate you as to the realities of the situation.

> **VIDEO TIP**
>
> For more information on our popular video course "FileMaker for Startups and Entrepreneurs", visit:
>
> http://bit.ly/LFentrepreneurs17

Notes from David (and endorsed by Richard)

If you want to build and sell a tool to FileMaker developers, there are a few things to keep in mind. Most FileMaker developers are too cheap to buy your product.

OK, that's not really it, but sometimes it seems that way to those of us who produce software for other FileMaker developers.

The truth is that there is a lot of stuff out there and the cost of those extras for FileMaker developers can quickly get out of control. As a result, the majority of FileMaker developers are extremely conservative in their buying decisions and generally purchase only what they absolutely must have.

Your wonderful and indispensable product will very likely be edged out by another wonderful product the developer needs slightly more than yours.

If you produce a product for use by other FileMaker developers, you should expect *not* to make any money on it. Yes, you will sell it, if it is good. But no, it is not likely you will sell enough copies to recover your cost of development.

The vast majority of such products never produce a meaningful profit for the developer. This includes even many of the best and most popular items that you probably thought, until now, were cash cows for their developers.

I know there are exceptions to this rule. One of those exceptions is 360Works and their SuperContainer product. Years before FMI learned that digital document management was necessary, the rest of the planet had already come to this conclusion. 360Works created a tool that allowed FileMaker developers to digitally store their documents in FileMaker, without destroying the performance of the FileMaker file. This was before remote containers.

360Works made a ton of cash every month selling this product, for a number of years. They delivered an absolutely critical solution that probably 85% of the FileMaker community needed and that FMI was unwilling to address. 360Works has also made a number of plugins that I have never used, because I do not consider them remotely critical to what I do.

If you decide to produce a product for other FileMaker developers, you must consider the cost of development to be the number of hours it takes you to produce it, multiplied by your standard hourly rate (plus any incidental expenditures). In this case, you are the client and you must pay the going rate for development. After all, if you weren't working on that software, you would have been working on something else that actually did produce that rate.

At this point you are no doubt asking yourself, *If all these tools and add-ons for FileMaker developers are not profitable, why are there so many of them?*

In 90% of cases they are tools the developer needed to create for his own use anyway. If you have to invest your own time and money in developing a tool to make your own work easier, you might as well get some of that investment back by selling it. However, there are some gotchas involved.

If you provide a product, you must service that product. Release a product, and no matter how good it is and how carefully you designed it, there will be bugs, support questions, email inquiries, product announcements to make and a host of other little attendant tasks. These cost you money because they take your time, if for no other reason. You can estimate spending roughly as much time on all of these other issues as you did developing the product in the first place, and that does not account for any outlays of real cash you may have to make promoting the product.

And then, there is the issue of upgrades… *Version 2* should already be in the beginning stages of development when you release *Version 1*.

All of these additional costs are a large part of the reason you will not make a profit on your FileMaker developer product.

Building a Vertical Market Product

Building a software package for a vertical market outside the FileMaker community is a different kettle of fish entirely… an old, hot, smelly kettle of fish that will not improve with age.

With exceptions that are rare, this is a *very* bad idea and for quite a number of reasons. I'm referring specifically to you the developer, building and marketing a vertical market product at your own expense, not to building a vertical market product for a client who will pay you for development and who intends to market the product himself.

Vertical market products are enormous money losers, nearly on par with high yield investment programs (otherwise known as scams). No, vertical market products are not scams, but you will feel like you have been scammed when you are done.

Most vertical market products require an enormous investment of both development time and actual money. Development time can be measured in months rather than days or weeks, and the cash outlay is usually substantial (advertising ain't cheap).

If you are reading this book, the odds are that you are a novice or intermediate developer. You may think that your idea for a vertical market software package is a sound plan, but you may be wearing rose-colored glasses. Let me tell you what happened to a friend of mine:

My friend was *not* a novice or intermediate developer. In fact he was one of the best and most respected developers in the FileMaker world. He made an impressive living building databases.

One day he decided to dive into the vertical market arena and invested roughly $500,000 in developing a product. The product was excellent. Extremely well designed and constructed, it performed quite well and filled a niche nicely. An added bonus was that my friend knew what he was doing when it came to marketing and sales. He had all the necessary skills to get the job done.

This was years ago and to this day he has not recovered even half of his investment.

If you are thinking of developing a vertical market product you should know that a high percentage, even the very best of them, fail. Either the market is not big enough, or an inferior product is already too entrenched to loosen its grip, or... who knows? The why's are not important. What is important is the fact that they do fail with alarming predictability.

When you have enough experience and skill under your belt to build a vertical market product that is of sufficient quality to be marketable, the odds are still heavily against you. Either don't do it at all, or bring in investors so that someone else is paying the freight. You would not take on a client who says; *There is a 5% chance I will pay you*. Why take yourself on as a client who essentially says the same thing?

If you are not a highly advanced developer and choose to dive into the vertical market pool anyway, be forewarned that this venture will very likely ruin you.

Releasing a product that is less than perfect will cause you to spend most of your time (and money) on bug fixes, upgrades, support calls, complaints, etc. while sales will not be high enough to cover all of those expenses. You will be forced to work full-time supporting software that does not pay you a living. With no free time for paying work, you will likely find yourself suddenly out of business!

If you are still determined to release a vertical market product, at least take this advice:

Find a skilled, established, and respected FileMaker developer of long standing and ask that developer to review your software and make recommendations with your vertical market goal in mind. This will probably cost you only a few hundred dollars and may save you many thousands. A wise investment.

There are many successful vertical market products; some of them are even big money makers. The people who hold the copyrights to those products may vehemently disagree with what I have said here, but successful vertical market software producers have a lot of skill, experience, and preparation going for them, and they probably lost money on the first several attempts they made at producing a successful product. If you cannot afford to lose the money, do not play!

One last consideration when you build a vertical market product with FileMaker you are automatically shot in the foot from the beginning and that's FMI's own bullet you feel. Unless you are selling a single-user product and can therefore build a stand-alone version of your solution, thereby eliminating the need for your customer to also buy a copy of FMP, you must convince buyers to purchase *both* your product *and* server, and individual FMP seats for each and every user.

When people buy Microsoft Office, for example, they do not expect to have to buy *other* software to make Microsoft Office work. They expect everything they need to be contained in one package at one price. They do not mind buying a separate word processor license for each user. They DO mind buying *two* licenses for each user (one for FMP and one for your product) in order to get what they see as one software product each.

FMI has attempted to remedy this situation by allowing vertical market developers to bundle FileMaker with their product. FMI has the SBA, Solution Bundle Agreement program.

In short, this program requires you to send in your solution for review by FMI. If the solution does not suck and FMI feels that the solution is a modern, good-looking application, then they will approve you into the SBA.

This allows you to buy FileMaker products at a highly discounted rate, with the sole intention that they are bundled with the sale of your vertical market application to the end-customer. The SBA program has some real benefits to it because it dramatically lowers the cost of FileMaker to your end client. But you will have to account for the cost of these discounted FileMaker products as part of your overall price.

FileMaker Certification

FMI offers a multiple choice certification test that is proctored internationally by Pearson Education Incorporated. Pearson is a third-party company that proctors a number of industry certification tests.

FMI continues to maintain a single certification test for each version of the FileMaker platform. Just because this test is multiple choice, it does not mean it's easy.

If you talk to the top FileMaker development companies, you are going to get two different sets of thoughts about the FileMaker certification test. One group of individuals sees the test as something that a senior developer with many years of experience should be able to pass using their knowledge they've gained over the years, with minimal studying. The other group is one which works to get their junior staff to pass the certification before they begin actually developing.

In my opinion, junior staff should never be expected to take and pass the certification test. I see the FileMaker certification test as a good checkmark towards verifying that a FileMaker developer has reached "senior status".

I can tell you, without a doubt, that a brand new Computer Science student with a four-year degree has no chance of passing unless they were given study materials specific to the test.

A huge section of the FileMaker certification test has to do with the ins and outs and subtleties of ODBC connections to an external data source like Oracle or SQL. This is a highly complex topic, and I do not allow any new hires/junior staff to assist on projects that require ODBC/SQL integration until they have proven themselves on lower level projects.

So how long does it actually take to become certified? If you are doing project work with real customers on a day-to-day basis, anywhere from four to seven years would be the timeline required to become legitimately certified.

API's Provided by FileMaker - For Senior Developers Only

If you are familiar with the XML or PHP API's provided by FileMaker, you may find the recently added "FileMaker Data API" (FDA) familiar. The "FileMaker Data API" (FDA) turns the FileMaker Server into a data source. It works on the same principle as XML or PHP API.

In practice, the FDA is similar to the XML API, rather than the PHP API. The PHP API comes with a library that hides the guts of the interactions behind a nice Object-Oriented interface. This can lead to some frustration if you're used to the PHP library. You may feel like your going backward if you try to "roll your own," instead of using a third-party REST API consumption library. However, the benefits do outweigh the downsides, given that there are plenty of robust libraries out there for exactly that reason.

And if you're a non-PHP developer looking to finally be able to talk to FileMaker without a ton of shenanigans, you're finally in luck, since the API is consumer-language agnostic!

What is it?

FileMaker's Data API was introduced in version 16, and has undergone some changes for 17. As an API, it is a way of getting data into and out of FileMaker. It also allows for a RESTful API, which means that it is designed to use the mechanisms of HTTP -- i.e. the standard HTTP verbs, headers, and responses. -- to transfer the state (if any) of the application representationally (ergo, REpresentational State Transfer, or REST). The HTTP verbs map to the CRUD actions. POST is **C**reate, GET is **R**ead, PATCH is **U**pdate, and DELETE is, well, **D**elete.

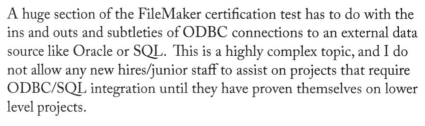

FILEMAKER JEDI REQUIRED

This FileMaker Jedi information Is great knowledge to have. However, it is a bit advanced so you may need to master all the other information in this book and come back to this section. This information is provided by Steve Allen, a Senior Engineer at RCC.

TERMINOLOGY

When a senior developer refers to words in all CAPS, ex: POST, GET, ect. they are referring to a Command.

Why is it important?

The FileMaker Data API makes FileMaker a full native citizen of the modern web, which is largely populated by services providing and consuming data via FileMaker Data API's.

How do I use it?

There is ample documentation of the FM Data API itself included with the Server installation. The link, by default is: https://[address of your FMS]/fmi/admin/apidoc/

However, this just explains what each call is. It doesn't explain the best methods for using the call in your particular app.

RCC recommends using an environment in Postman to test and develop your calls before using them in your app. This allows for clarity of vision, and assurance of expectations, without the "sausage-making" of getting your app to consume the API.

When it comes time to do the actual sausage-making, though, the Data API is so incredibly flexible. Most languages have several, if not a plethora of options to consume API's in an efficient and industry standard way for the specific language. Some quick internet sleuthing should reveal most of these. "Guzzle" for PHP is a great way to consume it, for one example.

Check out this link: http://docs.guzzlephp.org/en/stable/

Will it replace XML and PHP?

FileMaker says "yes." Given the expansion of the scope of possibility to any language, I think it will definitely become the standard, even to the point of finding the existing options obsolete.

However, the XML and PHP API's both allow for the direct use of Scripts. Currently, the Data API is capable of running Scripts, but only as a side effect, which is technically not "RESTful."

12 Critical Final Notes: Know Thyself & Know Thy Toolset

Reflect on the Reflection

This section is completely new in this release of the manual. It is a topic that started gurgling up as I was writing. There are a number of recurring themes in this book, and if you have read all the way through to this point, you have probably started seeing them yourself.

You may be a novice developer now, but your long-term goal may be to become a FileMaker professional. Unlike a lot of Hollywood and television-type personalities, who tend to be highly narcissistic, I am going to encourage you to look in the mirror. I want you to take an introspective look at yourself, as you address the issues and challenges identified in this book.

As I finish up writing, it occurs to me that a vast majority of the issues you are likely to see are self-inflicted issues. I want to encourage you to evaluate yourself objectively and be aware of these issues. This book has largely been an exercise in explaining these issues to you. My goal is to help you rectify those issues.

As you become aware of your weaknesses, you are less likely to repeat those problems. Some people spend a great deal of time complaining online about the FileMaker platform and how it is somehow broken.

The platform does have its fair share of weaknesses. However, you are likely to find that the biggest weakness in the platform is you. Yah. The truth hurts sometimes. It hurts me. I have made plenty of mistakes over the years. The trick is to learn from these.

Don't You Have Anything Positive to Say?

Most people who watch any of my videos are aware that I am very positive about the FileMaker platform. I spend a great deal of time talking about the tremendous number of awesome things that it does very well. It does a handful of things poorly, and of course, I am happy to address those as well. However, I want to be very clear so that I do not come off as a "Negative Nancy."

I see the vast majority of problems experienced by FileMaker developers as being self-inflicted issues. This book has largely been an exercise in explaining these issues to you. My goal is to help you draw conclusions on how to rectify those issues.

Over the years I have had the opportunity to get up and vent in front of senior FMI management. On more than one occasion, I have had the opportunity to address a large section of the company in a private presentation. In these settings, I used some four-letter words in addressing the issues with the platform.

For the most part, this book is pretty G-rated. While I would love to use spicy sentence enhancers (a SpongeBob Squarepants reference), my wife discourages this practice. However, in certain private settings, I have "let it rip" when I thought that FMI needed to hear the brutal truth.

I am pleased to say that a vast majority of the issues that I have vented about over the years have been addressed. A handful of critical issues remain, and FMI has publicly said that they plan to address these issues.

One issue remaining, is the fact that implementation of FileMaker Cloud is not a trivial exercise. FMI has indicated that they understand this and they would like to correct it.

In an ideal world, if you wanted to set up a database "in the cloud" all you would have to do is put in your name, username, and password (and probably your credit card). Once this is done, you would upload the FileMaker file that you want to be hosted. And you're done!

That, for me, is the ideal cloud implementation. We are not there yet.

The other major weakness of the FileMaker platform is relatively technical. If you have been playing with FileMaker for any period of time, you have probably noticed that it is pretty hard to copy/paste layouts, blocks of functionality, scripts, table occurrences, field definitions, etc. between two FileMaker files.

This lack of modularity, or the lack of being able to copy/paste structure and data from Point A to Point B, greatly impairs the platform. Developers need the ability to copy and paste code to successfully create shrink-wrapped products. The inability to copy and paste code greatly limits our ability to create patches or updates. There is no easy way for you to "fix some bugs" in a shipping version by just extracting out a quick patch and applying that patch to the live file. It does not work that way.

 As mentioned at the beginning of this book, FMI has made massive improvements to deployablility in the 17 release. FileMaker users (especially larger organizations) are often using a custom FileMaker app running on a dedicated FileMaker Server. This custom app would be considered the "live" or "production" database. In an ideal world, the FileMaker developer would be improving and modifying a separate copy of the database (aka "offline" or "dev file"). Once the work is completed, this Dev File would go through a process of testing and certification. Once it is tested, ideally the developer would press a button and the user's live database file is updated automatically.

In versions of FileMaker prior to 17, this process was a "super bitch" for a developer to complete. Many hours of wasted effort were spent trying to move the live production "data" into the new database.

The "FileMaker Data Migration Tool" (FDMT) changes this by rapidly moving data from the **live file**, to the **development file**. A process that used to take hours, now takes seconds.

We cover this tool in great detail in our video course. However, for most novice developers, this won't be something you'll deal with immediately. Most likely you are working in the most expedient way you know how; making edits to the live file. Given their novice skill set and the urgency of the work, this is just fine. (As long as you're working on a FMS or FMC with lots of backups).

As a developer becomes more experienced and the number of FileMaker users grow, they may want to consider using this process of working on an "offline" or "Dev File." This decision represents a trade-off in terms of benefits.

Pros/Cons of Work on a Live File:

Pro - Changes or fixes made to a live file immediately impacts the users. They are likely to benefit from this, and express their appreciation for you getting it fixed rapidly.

Pro - Customer can provide realtime testing and feedback

Pro - No need to move data from a Production File to a Dev File.

Con - A developer making major design changes to the schema of a FileMaker file has the potential to disrupt "live" FileMaker users. The screen may flash, or the user might have their layout forceably changed.

FYI

The FDMT is a command line driven tool. The "Evil Twins" at Productive Computing, have created a pretty user interface so you don't have to do the command line. You can find this tool at productivecomputing.com

Pros/Cons of Working on an Offline file - merging data at a specific date and time:

Pro - Major changes can be built and tested without disrupting the real users during their work day. Lower risk, since users won't be disrupted, or worse have their system break down due to bugs created by a developer.

Con - Getting the users to actually test an offline file can be a problem. Users don't want someone adding extra work to their schedule. A testing program needs to be established. Migrating users to an untested database will end badly for everyone.

Con - Migrating the data from the old file to the new file. This is now radically easier in FileMaker 17. But it still takes some effort.

FMI has stated in public forums that they will continue to improve these data migration capabilities. The 17 release is a great start. If they can fully address FileMaker's lack of robust support for upgrade/patching of solutions, that will just about negate the last of the major shortcomings of this platform. There are other issues of course, but frequently you can work around them.

All Is Not Lost

While FileMaker developers still face a couple of major limitations, FMI has been diligently addressing those issues. FMI is focused on making FileMaker flexible and modern.

I expect that FMI is on track to resolve the two major issues listed above. This is not some secret inside knowledge. This is information that has been publicly discussed by FileMaker Product Management teams. I expect this information to continue to make its way out to the public in the forthcoming year.

FYI

Rick Kalman (FileMaker's Director of Product Management and Design) has talked about Future design intentions on the FileMaker Community forum:

http://bit.ly/FMdesignforum17

What Makes a Good FileMaker Developer?

When I talk to my team about the overall critical skills to be a FileMaker developer, technical skills only account for one-third of the pile of tools that you need to have in your toolbox.

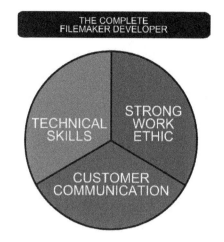

Great customer communication is another third. I would classify the number one source of problems for FileMaker developers as a lack of good communication with a customer. You can see that reflected in this book with a great deal of conversation focused on customer communication, testing, planning, and documentation.

The last third, of course, is a solid work ethic. I run into FileMaker developers that have wide-ranging levels of work ethic. I wonder how some people ever get out of bed in the morning. While at the opposite end of the spectrum, I meet some people and wonder if they ever sleep.

I really cannot help you with work ethic. There is an old axiom that says "you can lead a horse to water, but you can't teach it to drink." It is easy to show a person what a good strong work ethic is. It is up to them to get off of their ass and get moving.

The Social Side of the FileMaker Community

The FileMaker community is a unique collection of people that span a wide variety of businesses and skill sets. The FileMaker community is very big on providing help to fellow FileMaker users. You often see this reflected in free sample files and free assistance.

Even at RCC, we provide many free videos as well as free FileMaker solutions, like FM Starting Point. This is not unique to RCC.

When looking at the makeup of the FileMaker community, there are two types of FileMaker users. First off, there is the "in-house" person that inherited becoming a Filemaker developer. They are not full-time dedicated coders. They are people who typically have more than one job in an organization. They had their "day job" and then somewhere along the way, they got dumped into FileMaker development because they had to solve a problem. No one else at their company knew how to solve the problem. So, they built a FileMaker solution that fixed their company issue.

So, it is common to see that these people have their "regular day job," and also a FileMaker development job at the same time. These people are fundamentally going to be more sympathetic and helpful to other people in need.

The second FileMaker user is the full-time FileMaker developer. This is a person who pursued development as their career because they enjoy the problem-solving process. These people crave the creative process involved in solving business challenges. These people are also typically highly motivated individuals and this problem solving also spills over into their hobbies.

Typically these people crave working independently without an organizational structure. FileMaker developers tend to be people that get up in the morning whenever they want. They go to bed whenever they want. They are highly motivated to do project work and to solve problems creatively. Because of this, many developers will start their own one-man shop.

Frequently these people are highly social and so they are attracted to the social aspects of the FileMaker community. One reason is that they tend to not have a lot of social outlets in their one-man company. So, the FileMaker community provides great social benefits for these users.

FYI
Note to Readers from Editor: Richard like to use the term "socialness" to describe social behavior. We are not sure if this is a real word.

The high socialness can manifest itself in a variety of ways. If you ever go to a FileMaker event, like a FileMaker Developer Conference, probably more than half of the interactions will be in a social setting (eating, drinking, entertainment, outside of the actual conference, ect.).

Final Note

As we wrap up this edition of this text, I want to thank David Kachel for all of his hard work in generating the first versions of this document over the past ten years. David was gracious enough to pass the torch to me to allow the continuation of this text. I feel this manual is an excellent supplement to the existing video training that we already have with the FileMaker platform.

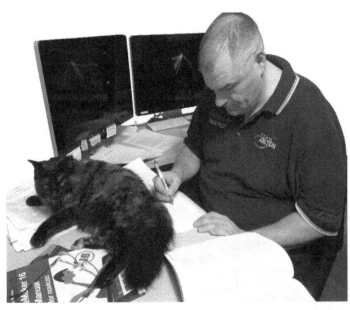

Frankly, I have admired this text for more than six years because I found that the original version very much subscribed to my experience and view of the FileMaker world.

If you have questions or comments about the book, please contact support@rcconsulting.com. If you want a digital version of this book, feel free to email our support team and tell us how much you love the book! For a couple of kind sentences, they will be happy to send you the PDF. Proceeds from this book will go towards buying treats for my fluffy kitties.

Additional Reading Material

FileMaker has discontinued a fairly decent training textbook. They previously updated this textbook with the help of consultants, over the last decade. But it was discontinued after the version 15 release. However, lots of good information can still be learned from the book.

FileMaker Training Series 15: http://www.filemaker.com/learning/archived-learning-resources.html

Other Video Resources

FileMaker has their very own super-basic introductory video course, which they call the FileMaker Custom App Academy:

http://www.filemaker.com/learning/custom-app-academy/

This course contains excellent, basic information, but It does not have the depth of our Pro video course. The Custom App Academy is about six hours in length. In comparison, there is a Lynda.com course that is about eight hours in length:

https://www.lynda.com/FileMaker-Pro-tutorials/Learning-FileMaker-16/569334-2.html

Our 17 platform video course at 55 hours in length offers even greater depth in training.

About the Author

Richard Carlton is a 28-year veteran of the FileMaker platform. He started building FileMaker solutions in 1990. Richard has a team of FileMaker developers spread throughout North America into approximately four major offices. Richard is best known for his prolific video courses on the FileMaker platform, as well as giving away the highly popular "FM Starting Point" business software (CRM). Richard has been a frequent speaker at the annual FileMaker Developer Conference and often provides free online webinars to answer critical questions about the FileMaker platform.

When Richard is not supporting the FileMaker platform, he is either spending time with his family or aviation, his two major interests. Richard has been known to drag various radio-controlled aircraft to FileMaker conferences, and he actually flew a large RC helicopter around the high-rise Marriott hotel in San Diego, California. Richard's wife tolerates his mayhem, and both of them love their seven rescue cats which mainly substitute for Richard's kids, who have all grown up and left the nest.

Special Contributors

Myles Debski is head of our Creative Services team at RCC. He has been with RCC for 10-years and taken on many roles. Myles drew most of the graphics in this book. He now has arthritis in both hands, since we began editing this book.

Michael Wallace is a certified senior engineer at RCC with over 10-years of FileMaker experience. He is well-versed and experienced in FileMaker as well as Web APIs. He shares his expertise and advice in a few sections of this book.

Nicolas Hunter spent 6-years at FileMaker as part of their User Interface Design team. Nick is the UI designer behind the current release of FM Starting Point, which is our free FileMaker business database. He has shared his professional advice and comments in a few sections of this book.

Steve Allen is a certified senior engineer, and has been with RCC for 14 years. He has a wide variety of successful customer projects. He has shared his knowledge in sections of this book.

Check Us Out

www.rcconsulting.com

www.learningfilemaker.com

www.fmstartingpoint.com

www.fmcoaches.com

www.fmcoachescorner.com

About the Original Author

David Kachel is a long-time FileMaker developer and owner of Foundation Database Systems. He started in FMP development with version 2 of FileMaker Pro™ way back in the CompuServe Claris Forum days where he was lucky enough to learn FileMaker programming from some of the very best in the business. If you find anything in this document that you consider particularly brilliant, it is reasonable to assume he learned it from others, as do we all. Remember to make your own contribution. David is now retired.

The FileMaker 17 Manual
for Novices